ADVENTURES
of a
TENNESSEAN

James Carl Duncan

authorHOUSE®

AuthorHouse™
1663 Liberty Drive
Bloomington, IN 47403
www.authorhouse.com
Phone: 1-800-839-8640

Published by AuthorHouse 6/13/2013

ISBN: 978-1-4817-4157-6 (sc)
ISBN: 978-1-4817-4156-9 (hc)
ISBN: 978-1-4817-4155-2 (e)

Library of Congress Control Number: 2013906899

FOREWORD

This volume contains the stories that were told to me as a young boy growing-up in Tennessee about the many adventures that my father experienced while serving in the United States Navy. The events and opinions contained within the individual stories represent those verbalized by my father. These stories contain rich and colorful language, and they reflect a United States Navy sailor's life during the mid-20th Century. My father, like all good story tellers, molded the events and experiences from his life into his stories to captivate the audience as well as create a larger than life version of what took place. Collectively, these stories provide insight into the thoughts and concerns of the generation of Americans that fought in the Korean armed conflict. I hope that you enjoy these adventures as much as I have.

ACKNOWLEDGEMENTS

For her assistance in proof-reading and all her work behind the scenes to help me prepare <u>Adventures of a Tennessean</u> for publication, I want to thank my wife, Brenda Duncan. Without her unwavering love and support, this book may not have been completed.

Also, I want to thank my Mother, Hazel (Strickler) Duncan, and my brothers and sisters, Linda (Duncan) Ware, Alvin Duncan, William Duncan, and Hazel Ann (Duncan) Swaw for their support and patience during the writing of this book.

DEDICATION

This book is dedicated to my father, Alvin Eunis Duncan, who was an incredible story-teller, outstanding teacher, and my hero. My father demonstrated why he was my hero on a hot summer day during the last week of July in 1969. School had been out for a couple of months, and I had been thinking about what it would be like to start high school (9th grade). As a soon to be freshman, I stood about 5 feet 4 inches tall, and I weighed about 140 pounds. On this particular day, I was helping my father mow the grass with a push mower. I was cutting grass in the area referred to as the gully run that was just to the East of my mother and father's home. As I was pushing the mower along the bank, it struck a piece of wire sticking out of the ground. Instantly, it felt like a cinder block had struck my right thigh. I let go of the lawn mower, and I stepped back lacing my fingers under my right thigh. As I pulled my thigh up, blood was spurting in an arc about two feet high from above my thigh. As I was to learn later, a piece of the wire over an inch long and a little smaller than a pencil in diameter had severed the main artery in my right leg and was lodged next to the bone. My father who was sitting on the back porch saw the blood spraying from my leg, and within seconds he was by my side. Dad picked me up like I was a rag doll, and he threw me over his shoulder. At the same time, he clamped his left hand over the wound on my thigh to stop the bleeding. Dad kept pressure on my thigh with his palm for about fifteen minutes before removing his hand. At the same time, he was talking to my mother about taking me to the hospital. When we arrived at Perry County Hospital, Doctor Gordon Turner came in and took x-rays of my thigh. He advised my father to take me to Vanderbilt Hospital in Nashville because they had a magnetic probe that might be able to pull the wire from my leg without further internal damage. Still dressed in blood covered clothing and with copies of the x-ray of my leg, my father and I headed for Vanderbilt Hospital. Once we arrived at Vanderbilt Hospital, we were ushered behind a curtain to await examination. Within minutes of my arrival, there was a young girl about 13 years old brought in on a stretcher who was pronounced dead on arrival. Her only injury was a small cut under her arm caused by a bicycle accident. This young girl had bled to death in less than five minutes because no one had stopped the bleeding. In sum, my father's quick thinking and actions had stopped the bleeding and saved my life.

TABLE OF CONTENTS

CHAPTER 1
JOINING THE NAVY

My name is Alvin Eunis Duncan, and I was born on July 31, 1930, in Perry County, Linden, Tennessee. Close family members called me by my middle name, Eunis. However, some friends and acquaintances referred to me by my nickname, Red. I received my nickname because of my curly, deep red hair. I was the oldest son of nine siblings born to James Alvin Duncan and Beulah Smith Duncan. At the age of 5, I started school at Middle Brush Creek Grade School, and I continued attending Middle Brush Creek Grade School until Perry County consolidated the schools. After consolidation, I attended Parnell Grade School on Coon Creek. In May of 1944, I graduated from the 8th grade at Parnell, and in the late summer of that same year, I started high school at Linden High School. May, 1948, proved to be the pivotal turning point in my life. This month was important not only because of my graduation from high school but also because of my induction into the Navy.

Looking back, the year 1948 had been very stressful for me because of the death of my father. My father, James Alvin Duncan, was a strong but gentle man. He was a descendant of the original Duncan's that had settled in the Tennessee River Valley before Tennessee had become a state. The land on which my father had lived his entire life was part of a ten thousand acre tract that had been in the Duncan family since the 1780's. No one but Duncans and Indians had lived on this land. After my father's death from pneumonia on the 6th of February, 1948, I became the man of the house. I had three younger brothers, Clarence Ezra Duncan, Scott Kirk Duncan, and Smith Thomas Duncan. I also had five sisters, Jewel Ida(Duncan) Kaskey, Ida Lorraine Duncan, Lottye Helen (Duncan) Rodgers, Jo Carolyn (Duncan) Lenk, and Beverly Joy (Duncan) Zimmerman. Of my sisters, Lorraine died at an early age, and Jewel and Helen were older than me. However, as the oldest son, the weight of earning money to help my family fell squarely on my shoulders.

My mother, Beulah Smith Duncan, was a very strong hard working woman. Like me, she had red hair. My mother's family had settled on Marsh Creek about fifteen miles west of Brush Creek. After my father died, mother did her best to hold the family together and to provide a firm foundation for the younger children to go out into the world on their own.

By late April of 1948, the fields that I had planted on the home place were coming alive with young tender corn shoots about three inches high. The entire Duncan family and my close relatives had been very happy about my graduation from Linden High School in Perry County. Upon graduation, I stood six feet tall, and I weighed approximately 165 pounds. During high school, I played point guard for the Linden High School basketball team under the famous coach, Willie Hudson. Few men had the eye hand coordination that I had. My eye hand coordination had developed after years of using an axe to cut down trees and split firewood. Graduating from high school was considered a major accomplishment in Tennessee at that time, but there was no pot of gold waiting for me upon graduation.

In 1948, jobs in Perry County were as scarce as hen's teeth. The economy of Perry County had not recovered from the Great Depression of the 1930's, when men worked ten hours a day for as little as a dime an hour. During the 1930's, men would stand waiting for work around the sawmills. Each hoping that someone would quit or get hurt so that they could take their place. From these back breaking jobs, most of the men barely earned enough to support their families. By 1948, the hourly wage had improved, but no jobs were available. Even today, the economy in Perry County remains stagnant relying primarily on the saw milling industry and farming.

My tour of duty in the United States Navy began on the 17th of May, 1948, and continued until the Korean War Armistice Agreement was signed on July 27, 1953. Initially, I had planned to join the Air Force. I had completed all the paperwork to join the Air Force, and I was scheduled to leave on the 20th of May, 1948, for an Air Force induction physical in Nashville, Tennessee. Little did I know how soon this was to change.

On weekends, as was the custom on Brush Creek, I would walk down Upper Brush Creek Road to the local country store located on Tennessee State Highway 100 to visit with my friends and to listen to the local gossip. While sitting in the country store talking with my friends, Billy Hayes Qualls indicated that he had signed up to join the United States Navy. Billy was my second cousin. His family lived about a mile west of my family on Brush Creek. Almost everyone on Brush Creek and Coon Creek was related to me in some manner. During the conversation, I indicated that I had signed up to join the United States Air Force. Neither Billy nor I really had any preference as to which branch of service we joined. So while sitting there swapping lies, one thing led to another until Billy and I decided that we should both join the same branch of the service. To decide who would go with whom, we decided to match one another. The wager basically was, if I won Billy would go into the United States Air Force with me, and if Billy won, I would go into the United States Navy with him. I lost the wager, so rather than leaving on

3

the 20th of May as planned, I had to leave on Monday the 17th of May, 1948, with Billy.

Billy was joining the military service because he was old enough to be drafted, and he had decided rather than be drafted into the United States Army that the United States Navy would be safer. Although Billy was two years older than me, he lacked my flare for leadership among the young men in the local community. In effect, Billy and the other young men normally followed my lead. My reason for joining the military service was simple. I needed a job. Faced with the job outlook in Perry County, I looked beyond Perry County for work. In addition, I craved the adventure that the military service promised. It was in this frame of mind that I originally signed up to join the United States Air Force.

At the time that I entered the United States Navy, I was seventeen. Before I could join the Navy, my mother had to sign a consent form. Mr. Thomas Beasley, who lived on middle Brush Creek in Perry County, was a Navy recruiter at the time. As luck would have it, Mr. Beasley happened to be in Perry County the weekend prior to the 17th of May, and he helped me fill out the initial paper work to join the United States Navy.

As planned, Billy and I left early on Monday, the 17th of May for the Nashville recruit center which was over eighty miles north and east of our home town of Linden, Tennessee. Billy and I had to be at the United States Navy recruit center in Nashville at 7:00 A.M. Upon reaching the Navy recruit center, I was taken to a room to have my paperwork and physical for induction completed. Billy and the other recruits who had completed their induction paperwork and medical physical exam during an earlier visit were taken into another room. When it came time for Monday's new recruits to be sworn in under oath, only the recruits who had completed their medical physical exam and induction paperwork prior to arriving in Nashville were permitted to be sworn in. The other recruits like me, who had not completed the medical physical exam and induction paperwork, were placed in the adjoining room to receive a physical exam while the others were sworn in.

When I joined the Navy, I signed up for what was called a Minority Cruise. A Minority Cruise was billed as a three year tour. This three year tour ultimately changed because of the start of the Korean conflict. President Harry S. Truman involuntarily extended all service members for a couple of years to fight the North Koreans. Service during the Korean War became a badge of honor for me.

As I often mentioned to those who had not served in the United States armed forces, you never forget your military service number. I received my military service number at the recruit center in Nashville. Today, military service numbers like the one I received are no longer used. In the current armed forces, military members use their social security number as their military service number. When I volunteered for the United States Navy, military service numbers were a necessary evil for keeping track of a military members pay, leave, awards, punishments, and training. My military service number was similar to the current requirement for all United States citizens to have and use their social security number for record keeping. Today, the social security number and the computer are the new tools that the United States Government uses to keep track of all Americans. These tools work just like the military service number that I was issued in May, 1948.

After induction into the United States Navy, I left Nashville that same day with all the new recruits. We were headed for boot camp in San Diego, California. It took seven days by train to cross the country. On the first night, we arrived in Dallas, Texas, but from Dallas forward travel to San Diego became a nightmare. The train that I left Nashville on the 17th of May was a fine train, but in Dallas, Texas, we all changed over to a second train. The second train, although a Pullman like the first train, turned out to be more like a cattle car. I remember sitting with the other recruits for over seventeen hours on the tracks before being transferred to the second train. On this second train, we traveled to El Paso, Texas. The blowing sand outside the train would pass right through the walls. There was sand in our bunks, sand in our clothes, sand in our food, and sand in the air. Upon reaching El Paso, we waited on the tracks for two days in the hot sun for a third train to arrive. Sitting inside the second Pullman train for two days without air conditioning or water was not a pleasant experience. To get a drink of water, I had to buy water in the local cantina. This was the first time that I had ever had to buy water to drink. Meal tickets were distributed to all recruits so that we could obtain three meals a day in the local cantina. The sandy food provided by the cantina reminded me of the mud pies children make when playing. This food was barely better than nothing at all.

Finally, on the fifth day, all recruits boarded the third train for the last leg of the journey to San Diego, California. This train went around the Rocky Mountains by going south almost into Mexico before entering California. From each of these three trains, I stared out the windows at the countryside. It was the first time that I had seen the western United States. I was surprised to find that the land from El Paso, Texas, to western California was semi-arid high desert with very little difference in the vegetation. From my perspective, it was as if the artist who had painted the United States had run out of green paint once he left El Paso, Texas.

When we arrived in San Diego, California, buses were waiting. From the train station, we were loaded like cattle onto the buses and taken to the training center at San Diego. At the training center, I received my first real taste of Navy efficiency by going through another complete medical physical examination. I still recall the Navy corpsman in San Diego saying, "Pee in this bottle, draw blood here, do this, and do that." Upon completion of this second medical physical examination, while I and the other recruits were naked as plucked birds, we were lined up for shots. No one told us what kind of shots we would receive. Being curious I moved to a position where he could see what was happening. It appeared that every time a recruit received a shot, he would just keel over. After keeling over, two Navy corpsmen would pick up the unconscious man and carry him into the next room. Behind me in the shot line, there was a big burly man who seemed to be in a hurry. In hindsight, I realize that this man was starving for attention. To obtain this attention, the big burly man would clown around. I do not remember this big man's name, but I do remember how the big man kept pushing and shoving me and others in front of him. When it came to pushing and shoving, I was like a mule. In front of me was the unknown, and I really did not want to go into the room where they were knocking men out with this shot. When I got up to the door, I could see a Navy corpsman with a big needle. Suddenly, the big man behind me started pushing again, and almost like a reflex action, I reached back and pulled the big burly man up in front of me and shoved him into the room. Just as the big man entered the room, the Navy corpsman shot him with the needle. The big man turned as white as snow and just fell over like he was dead. I later learned from the doctor that the shot we were given was for Cholera. Since I was next in line, I walked in, and the corpsman stuck me with a needle. After the shot, I stood there looking for a soft place to fall, but I did not pass out. I looked at the doctor, and I asked him, "When will I pass out?" The doctor replied, "Not everyone passes out, Red." I replied, "Everyone that I have seen take this shot has passed out." The doctor said, "Red, go on into the next room." When I went into the next room, I saw that not everyone was passing out.

After the Cholera shot, all recruits were divided alphabetically into different companies. Each company was assigned a barracks, and we were issued military gear and uniforms. We were told to use our mattress covers as sacks to carry the issued military gear and uniforms. By the time I received all my military gear and uniforms, I had a mattress cover full of items. With my mattress cover stuffed full, I struggled to carry these items to my assigned barracks. No transportation was provided to assist with this movement. It was an ugly sight to see over one hundred men in my company stretched out for about half a mile as we tried to carry our stuff to the barracks. However, I will say that this was the last time my company ever walked in an undisciplined manner. To my amazement, within two weeks, the drill instructors had molded my company into a sharp marching outfit.

CHAPTER 2
BOOT CAMP TRAINING

As luck would have it, Billy and I were both assigned to Basic Recruit Training Company 165. This resulted in Billy and I going through boot camp together in San Diego, California. As I look back at boot camp, this training could best be described as a form of mental and physical conditioning, which instills discipline and prepares young recruits to bond together as a cohesive unit. To help develop this cohesive bond, my drill instructors utilized an internal form of discipline known as peer pressure. Due to its effectiveness, peer pressure probably will continue to be used as the tool of choice to change the mind set of raw recruits and to develop a well-disciplined military force. As I learned, the stage must be set for peer pressure to work. First, raw recruits must be separated from family and friends, and their individualism must be suppressed. Next, the drill instructors must create group punishments for the errors of a single recruit and teach recruits to rely on one another for success. Throughout boot camp, my drill instructors relentlessly stressed team work, praised uniformity, and frowned upon individualism.

Billy and I were among the first recruits to be sent through a new eight week boot camp training course which the Navy had established in San Diego. In the past, boot camp lasted sixteen weeks, they condensed this training to eight weeks. We finished everything that the sailors before us had done in sixteen weeks in eight. To accomplish this, Company 165 ran day and night. Many of the sailors going through boot camp with me did not even have a place to sleep. Some of those in my platoon including me did not have a rack to sleep in so we slept on the porch of the barracks at night. No sleeping bags were available, but we were issued two blankets, one to lay down on the floor and a second to cover up with. Every morning, I would pick up my two blankets, fold them, and put them inside my sea bag which was in the corner of the barracks.

During boot camp, I was selected to be the platoon leader of second platoon because of my leadership, physical endurance, and superb eye hand coordination. Being a boot camp platoon leader is a position that no one in his right mind should want, and if I had it to do over, there is no way that I would let them make me a boot camp platoon leader. The drawbacks simply out weigh the advantages. For example, when it came to standing duty at night, all recruits had to stand a two hour watch, except the boot camp platoon leader who stood a four hour watch. While on watch the platoon leader did not get to stay in the barracks, the platoon leader had to walk from the barracks to the headquarters building and back to the barracks to make a report every hour. In sum, every hour the platoon leader would walk at least two miles. In addition, the boot camp platoon leader was required to make an hourly inspection of every floor to include the outside of the barracks. By the time, the platoon leader had completed his four hour duty, he had walked over eight miles. After standing a four hour watch at night in addition to the normal training activities of boot camp, I was worn out. Furthermore, the platoon leader would receive duty more frequently because there are not as many noncommissioned officers (NCOs as they call them) as there are enlisted. About every other night, the boot camp platoon leader would get to stay up half the night on duty walking back and forth to the headquarters. In short, as the boot camp platoon leader, I was worked to a frazzle.

While at boot camp, my company became known as the meatball company of our battalion. A meatball company is a company that is proficient at drill, marksmanship, and combat skills. To become a meatball company, a company had to win at least four pennants during competitions with the other companies, which were going through boot camp training. My company was the best at drill, marching, marksmanship, and combat skills. As a result, we won all the pennants. There were benefits to being a meatball company. As the meatball company, our company was able to move to the head of the chow line, movie line, and church line. Our unit marched everywhere: to chow, to the movies, to church every Sunday, and to every training class or field exercise.

As part of boot camp, all recruits were required to qualify with a rifle on the firing range. On the firing range, I had qualified as an expert not only with a rifle but also with the pistol. My ability to shoot a rifle started at an early age in Perry County, Tennessee. At home, it was my job to hunt wild game to help feed the family.

At the boot camp rifle range, several sailors in my battalion failed to qualify. Some of those who failed to qualify with the rifle thought that they could be discharged from the United States Navy by failing to qualify with the rifle. Likewise, some refused to learn how to swim under the mistaken belief that they would be discharged from the Navy.

As an additional duty in boot camp, I was saddled with the job of taking the sailors in my company and the other companies who had failed to qualify with the rifle out to the range for requalification. For requalification, I had to take these sailors to the rifle range on the Marine Base at Camp Pendleton.

Trying to get these sailors qualified, when they did not want to qualify, seemed an impossible task. I had taken the same sailors out to the range on three separate occasions, and each time these sailors had gone unqualified (UNQ). On the fourth trip out with these sailors, a big Marine Sergeant came up to me and said, "Red, if you were over there in that pill box, with a good shooting M-1 rifle, with plenty of ammunition, and with a telephone, and if that phone were to ring, and someone were to say that they needed a couple of bulls eyes on a certain target, do you think that you could make it happen?" I looked at the Marine Sergeant and said, "Possibly." After this conversation, I made my way over to the pill box. Sure enough there was an M-1 rifle and plenty of ammo. I had not been in the pill box long when the phone rang. The person on the phone indicated that target number 5 needed three bulls eyes to qualify. I sighted in and put three bulls eyes in target 5. I laid in the pill box a few more minutes, and I received another call. Once again, I provided a couple of bulls eyes to qualify another sailor. We were doing pretty well. There was just one problem. It became boring. To amuse myself, I started watching the disks that the Marines in the range butts were using to indicate the shooter's score on his last shot on his target. The disks being used to indicate each shooters score looked about the size of the head of a match from my location in the pill box. Before I knew it, I began to follow the disks with the rifle, and I thought to myself, "I wonder if I could hit one of the marking disks." Finally, my curiosity got the best of me, and I shot at one of the marking disks. What happened next was comical. When I shot the marking disk, it stood there shaking for a couple of seconds and went straight down. I lay there a couple more minutes and another disk went up, and I shot it. I was having a great time! All of a sudden, I felt this tremendous weight on the back of my shoulders. I could hear the individual standing on my shoulders cursing me. I managed to turn my head, and I saw the Marine Sergeant who had spoken to me earlier standing on my shoulders cursing a blue streak. The Marine Sergeant was saying, "I should have known that it was you shooting the disks."

As punishment for shooting the disks, I was assigned to pull targets in the butts for one week on the Marine rifle range detail. Working in the butts was an education. In the butts, we stapled cheese cloth to wooden frames on which we attached targets. These wooden frames were fastened to manually operated carriages. On this particular range, there were fifty carriages all lined up in a row. When a carriage was up, the target in the carriage was raised above the protective berm becoming visible to the shooter. Each shooter on the rifle range was assigned a separate target, and in the butts at least one Marine or sailor was assigned to raise and lower the carriage containing the target of each shooter. When working in the butts not only did you have to raise and lower your assigned carriage in accordance with appropriate range commands, but you also had to mark all shots, which struck your target and disk the shooter's score after each shot. To accomplish this job, required the butt pullers to remain alert and to watch their target and the berm behind their target closely for shot impacts. If you saw a shot strike your target or the berm behind your target, you immediately pulled your carriage down, marked the location where the shot struck the target with a spotter. The spotter used to mark the location of the shot impact on the target had to be the opposite color in order to be visible. This allowed the shooter to see the portion of the target where the shot hole appeared, for example, white on black. After spotting the shot location, the carriage was raised and the shot was disked. The disk, which we used, was a flat, round piece of wood connected to a long handle. The round part of the disk was about fifteen inches in diameter. The handle was about six feet long. It resembled a giant lollipop. The disk was red on one side and white on the other. To signal a bulls-eye (five points), the round portion of the disk was placed over the bulls-eye portion of the target so that the white side of the disk was visible to the shooter when the target was in the raised position. A four was indicated by placing the disk over the bulls-eye portion of the target so that the red side of the disk was visible to the shooter. A three was shown by placing the disk on the right side of the target as the butt puller faced the target so that the red side was visible to the shooter. To indicate a two, the disk was placed on the left side of the target as the butt puller faced the target so that the red side was visible to the shooter. A miss was signaled by passing the disk from left to right as the butt puller faced the target so that the red side of the disk was visible to the shooter. Disking a miss was known as waving "Maggie's Drawers."

In the butts, I was a fast learner. Making targets was easy. To make a target you simply glued a target sheet to the cheese cloth covering the wooden target frame. The cheese cloth gave the target the strength to withstand the wind and also to provide a background surface to hold shot spotters. The Marines that I worked with in the butts were good men. When I was off duty from the range detail, I would go with these Marines to different locations on Camp Pendleton. It was during this time that I had the opportunity to meet one of the Marine Corps' best match shooters. This shooter was an egotist who felt that he was too good to associate with the Marines who worked in the butts. I would describe him as an individual full of his own self-importance. He felt that the individuals working in the butts were peons.

One day while I was working in the butts, this super Marine Corps shooter came out to the range for target practice. This was a big mistake. I switched places with the Marine who was pulling the target for this super Marine shooter. When the super Marine shooter fired his next shot, instead of marking the bull's eye, which he fired, I put a shot spotter down in the lower left hand corner of the target, pasted up the shot hole in the bull's eye and disked him "Maggie's Drawers." This super Marine shooter shot again cutting the heart out of the bull's eye. Again, I pulled the target. This time, I placed a spotter in the upper left hand corner, pasted up the shot hole in the bull's eye, and disked him a miss waving "Maggie's Drawers." From other Marines in the butts, I received word that this super Marine shooter was adjusting the windage and elevation on his M-1 rifle. I was just rolling in the butts. The focus of all the Marines on the range was on this great Marine Corps shooter who had been disked two misses.

After he adjusted his sights, I did not have to make a fake shot hole because he really did miss the target. His shooting really was messed up. I was having a great time playing with this stuck up super Marine Corps shooter. About two shots later, the big Marine Sergeant who had me assigned to the range detail showed up in butts with a big cigar in his mouth. When he saw me pulling the target for the Marine Corps' super shooter, he knew what had happened. He started cussing me and jumping up and down, but it was too late. I already had that super Marine shooter where he could not hit the broad side of a barn.

The Marine Sergeant said, "Now you will have two more weeks on the range detail." For the next two weeks, this Sergeant put me on the ammo hauling detail. He would not let me go back into the butts anymore. On the ammo detail for the range, I had to drive the jeep hauling the ammo. Each morning, I had to park the jeep outside the ammo dump by 4:00 A.M. in the morning. The Marines at the ammo dump would load the jeep with ammo while I was eating breakfast. Around 5:00 A.M. I would return from breakfast, sign for the ammo, and drive the ammo out to the range. By following this procedure, the Marines were able to have the ammo passed out to the shooters and start firing at first light, which occurred between 5:30 A.M. and 6:00 A.M. depending on the cloud coverage.

While I was hauling ammo the first week, the black Marine,

who had been signing me out with the ammo, hung himself. On the morning of his suicide, I had parked the jeep at 4:00 A.M. at the ammo dump, and when I returned at 5:00 A.M., I found him hanging from the ceiling of the ammo dump. To me it seemed that his neck had been stretched till it was about a foot long. Not until that time, had I known anyone who had committed suicide. Observing a suicide victim is not a good way to start one's day.

Each morning, while I was hauling ammo, I could hear Marines chanting over in the distance. I did not know whether the Marines chanting on the distant hills had not made it in from the night before or whether they had gotten a very early start that morning. On the range detail, I tried to get my week's work finished by Friday at 3:00 P.M. so that I was ready for liberty. However, the leathernecks that I worked with on the range detail did not get off for liberty until noon on Saturday.

While waiting for my Marine buddies on that first Saturday, I stood out of sight behind the Marine Commander where I could see the Marines whom I worked with on the range detail. My buddies were standing in formation. Since I enjoyed tormenting and teasing these Marines, I tried to make them laugh by making faces at them while they stood in formation. On this Saturday morning, they had just returned from a twenty mile march with a full pack. A Master Sergeant walked down the front of the formation. He turned, looked at one of my buddies and asked, "Are you tired?" My friend said, "No, sir." The Master Sergeant asked, "Why not?" My buddy responded, "Because I am a Marine, Sir." When I heard him say this, I almost died laughing. After this formation, my Marine buddies were given liberty. I was given liberty too, but with one drawback, I had to wear a Marine uniform on liberty. Luckily, on Friday evening I had located a Marine my size who was willing to allow me to wear his jacket, and I borrowed a pair of trousers from another Marine. Dressed in a Marine uniform, I made a striking appearance. Feeling mischievous just outside the gate at Camp Pendleton as we left on liberty Saturday afternoon, I turned to my buddy and said, "Are you tired? No, Sir. Why not? Because I am a Marine." With this statement, I was able to initiate the response that I wanted as these Marines chased me all the way to Oceanside. I really had a great time aggravating the Marines on the range detail. If I had stayed on the range detail for another thirty days, I probably would have driven them nuts.

After graduation from boot camp, I came home on leave to Perry County, Tennessee. When I joined the Navy, I made fifty dollars a month whether I wanted it or not. After boot camp, I received a raise boosting my pay to fifty-five dollars a month. All my family and friends were impressed with my stories about the Navy. On the 31st of July, 1948, my birthday, I headed back to San Diego, California, to report for a special engineering school that had been developed for enlisted United States Navy personnel.

CHAPTER 3
ENGINEERING SCHOOL

B ased upon my test scores in mathematics and science, I was selected to attend follow-on training at a three week engineering class in San Diego, California. Billy Qualls and another sailor named Fisher from our Recruit Training Company 165 were also selected to attend this engineering class. During this three week introductory engineering course, my academic performance as well as the performance of Fisher was outstanding. Fisher and I were like sponges. We soaked up the basic engineering principals presented, and we academically led the class. Because of our enthusiasm and superb performance in this introductory engineering course, Fisher and I were chosen to continue our training in the field of engineering at an advanced training course in Cincinnati, Ohio, which started on the last week of September, 1948.

The advanced engineer training course was known as a Class C Engineering School. At this school, years of training on engineering topics were condensed into a six week period of instruction covering the basic theories and their application to the Navy's major areas of concern. In this school, we covered the equivalent of what was taught in a college level course on the following topics: electricity, refrigeration, gas engines, diesel engines, steel work and welding, plumbing and pumps, and ship design. For example, in the steel work and welding segment, Fisher and I studied different welding, soldering, and cutting techniques to include under water welding.

With the smell of Fall in the air in late September, we started the Class C Engineering School. Since it was still quite warm in the evenings, Fisher and I studied outside sitting at a picnic table almost everyday after class. To provide refreshment during our study sessions, Fisher and I would have a fifth of Jack Daniel's whiskey sitting on the table. For hours, we would sit on the picnic table going over the engineering principles that had been covered by the instructors that day. At times Fisher and I would leave class totally frustrated because we had no idea what the instructor had been talking about. Often we did not understand the different mathematical formulas or how to use them. Like me, Fisher had not been exposed to trigonometry or to these engineering principles in high school. Everything that we covered was new to us.

Luckily for Fisher and me, there was a very intelligent and helpful librarian at this advanced engineering school. If it had not been for this librarian, Fisher and I would not have learned enough to successfully complete this Class C Engineering School. This librarian patiently taught us how to use the library and how to apply the different engineering formulas to our homework problems. In addition, she helped us locate books and materials which explained in more detail the different engineering principles that we were covering.

As I look back on this training now, it seems that Fisher and I were the only ones who were doing any studying. In the evenings while we were studying, an older gentleman who also was attending this engineering school would stop by to chat with us. Almost without exception he would end up drinking most of our whiskey, and then he would disappear inside the engineer training classroom building. One evening when he came by, we did not have any whiskey. He wanted to know why we did not have any whiskey, and I said to him, "By God, you could have brought some. They sell it to anybody." The next day when we were sitting outside studying, he came by with a bottle of whiskey.

During this advanced engineer training class, Fisher and I developed a great friendship. Our hard work and study paid off as we both successfully completed this training. Upon graduation, Fisher and I received orders to report back to San Diego, California. For travel time from the engineering school to San Diego, the United States Navy gave Fisher and I fourteen days. The day after graduation, Fisher and I were on a train headed west. On this train, we ran into the older gentleman who came by to drink whiskey with us on the picnic table at the advanced engineering school. During the ensuing conversation, we learned that we were going to split up in Louisville, Kentucky. Fisher and the older gentleman who drank whiskey with us were going to transfer to different trains, one headed to the northwest and the other to the southwest. Fisher was going to visit his family in Idaho before returning to San Diego, and the older gentleman was traveling straight to San Diego and on to the naval bases in Hawaii. I on the other hand was headed south to Nashville and on to Perry County to visit my family before traveling to San Diego.

On the train ride from Cincinnati, each of us had drunk a lot of whiskey. Because our group was splitting up to go our separate ways, the older gentleman gave Fisher and me one of his cards. Written on this card was United States Navy Admiral. I read the card, and I looked at him and said, "Are you in the Navy?" The minute that it came out I wished that I could have put it back in my mouth, but it was too late. There I was holding his card, which said that he was an Admiral in the United States Navy, and I had asked such a foolish question. He said, "Yes, and if there is ever anything that I can do for you, come see me." I was so embarrassed that I could have walked under the rug on the train floor. Without knowing it, Fisher and I had gone to school with Rear Admiral Rodgers.

After brief visits with our families, Fisher and I reported to San Diego. In San Diego, we were ordered to the naval yards where ships were repaired. At the naval yards, Fisher and I were tested for yard certification. To become yard certified, you had to understand and demonstrate the welding techniques, cutting techniques, plumbing (to include valve operations and piping functions), and ship design principles. Fisher and I had no problem obtaining our yard certifications. Without question, we had mastered the knowledge needed to be yard certified.

After Fisher and I became yard certified, we thought that we would be working in the naval yards in San Diego. During this period, Fisher and I had been billeted in the naval barracks in Coronado, California. The barracks on Coronado had been constructed quickly during World War II. Sometimes building something quickly results in poor quality, which was exactly what happened with the barracks in Coronado. The primary construction material used in these barracks was Beaver Board. Every time a minor earthquake would strike southern California, the barracks would sway back and forth.

While waiting for our expected permanent assignment to the naval yard in San Diego, Fisher and I felt that we were leading the "Life of Riley." Not since joining the Navy had there been a time that we were not assigned specific duties. After receiving our yard certification, all we did was clean the barracks, eat, and go to the movies. We thought that we had it made. Our so called "Life of Riley" lasted about four days. This four day period seemed like a life time because during that period we did not have officers or senior petty officers breathing down our necks.

CHAPTER 4
UNDERWATER DEMOLITION TEAM

I was a member of the first Underwater Demolition Team (UDT), which existed in the United States Navy. During the past 65 years, the UDT changed and evolved. Today, members of the UDT would be known as members of the United States Navy's Sea Air, Land (SEAL) Teams, commonly referred to as the United States Navy SEALs. Little did I know that the UDT would morph into the United States Navy's principal special operations force and would become a part of Naval Special Warfare Command.

How I came to be a part of that first UDT unit is unclear even to me. Neither Fisher nor I volunteered, and as to how the other sailors in our class were selected, I have no idea. I attribute my selection to being in the wrong place at the wrong time. The following common traits seemed to apply to all the sailors in our UDT class: physical fitness, mental sharpness, maturity, and resilience. I always felt that someone in the United States Navy secretly screened the candidates for this first class to determine their potential to succeed. My memory of the UDT seems like a distant bad dream, which began when a Senior Chief Petty Officer came to the barracks in Coronado, California, and told Fisher and me that we were going to be tested for a swimming class. At first, Fisher and I had a ball in this swimming class. As the so called swimming class progressed, the Navy revealed that this class was the start of a new Special Forces Unit.

Once we were told that we were training for a Special Forces Unit everything happened fast. In my mind, it seemed like one day we were swimming, relaxing, without a care in the world, and then all of a sudden we were training for the UDT. None of us knew what work was until UDT training started. Training for this new unit was relentless. Our UDT training began in late October, 1948, outside Coronado. The training we received was designed to test our spirit and stamina. The first phase of our training dealt with physical conditioning, which focused on running, swimming, navigating obstacle courses, and basic under water skills. The physical conditioning training consisted of a very rigid exercise program designed to tax our physical endurance and will power. On a typical day, the UDT instructors had us up at 4:00 A.M. to go on a five mile run. Upon our return, we took what was called a physical training (PT) shower. A PT shower was a shower, which lasted less than three minutes from start to finish. After showering, we double timed to breakfast. Unlike the sailors stationed in San Diego, we did not go through a regular chow line. Instead, we marched into a special wing of the chow hall, which contained two long tables. After being seated at these tables, mess men would bring in our food. A typical breakfast would consist of platters of steak, ham, fried potatoes, biscuits, fried eggs, scrambled eggs, pitchers of milk and water, jars of jelly, and plates of butter. We ate like kings compared to the other sailors in the chow hall. For the breakfast meal, we were given fifteen minutes to eat from the time our unit reached the chow hall until we were to be in formation to leave.

Usually following breakfast, our unit would receive detailed class instruction on one of several topics, which had to be mastered before graduation. These classes included: diving, under water welding and cutting, repelling, hand to hand combat, explosives handling, and small arms training. To emphasize the material covered in these periods of instruction, our unit would receive class demonstrations. After these demonstrations, we would go back to physical training. Initially, our daily routine included swimming at noon; however, the physical training increased until we were spending approximately eight hours each day swimming and exercising.

My class contained 100 sailors when we started UDT training. During the second day of UDT training, the head instructor told us to look around at the others in the class. There was total silence as all of us looked at those sitting near us wondering if this was some kind of a test. Then with a deep growl he barked, "Only one out of five of you will complete UDT successfully." None of us believed this statement. Ultimately, his prediction proved to be too optimistic as only 17 of those in my class graduated. I look back on this statement about the dropout rate and wonder whether it was a form of psychology used by the head instructor to make us strive harder. Since I had just turned eighteen, I was gullible. Needless to say this statement about the drop out rate had a profound impact on me. Because of this statement, when I was hurting, sore, or tired, I masked it. I was determined to succeed. In fact, Fisher and I would not have quit even if our lives had depended on it. As Fisher and I built up our stamina and physical endurance, we would laugh at the instructors and challenge them.

In the beginning, our swimming for UDT was done in a swimming pool. This swimming pool was larger than an Olympic size pool and ten feet deep. However, our UDT class soon learned that this was not a normal pool. After our first week of swimming, the instructors changed the rules. The new rules were that once you got into the pool, you could not get out. To prevent us from getting out, special boards were placed on the sides of the pool. These boards were covered with a slick, ceramic coating so that you could not hang onto them. After the first week, entry into the pool became an all day affair (8 hours). I got to the point that I could put my hand out like a suction cup to hold onto the slick wall of the pool.

Upon completion of the swimming pool phase of our training, we were taken out to sea. Usually, our unit would be dumped out over twenty miles from shore. It can be unnerving to be dumped out in water where no land is visible. For safety purposes small boats were present to rescue those men who had problems. In this environment, our instructors would come by with a small boat as fast as it would run with a life ring extended from a boom on the side of the boat. The life ring would be just above the water. The objective was for us to grab the ring as the boat came by. After grabbing the ring, the boom holding the ring would rotate around to the rear of the small boat where we would roll up a ramp and climb into the boat. The only problem was that when you grabbed the life ring with the boat traveling at 30 knots or better, it would almost jerk your arm out of its socket. If you managed to hold on, you would be skimming along the water just like a skipping stone. I soon learned that skimming along the top of the water would burn you just like being dragged along a road. It did not take me long to figure out that the trick was to miss the life ring deliberately without letting them know that you had missed it on purpose. When you missed the life ring, they had to slow down and turn around to come back. After slowing down to turn around, they could not get the boat going as fast so you could grab the ring and get on board. The purpose behind using the boat and ring was to pick us up after an operation when the enemy was shooting at us.

As the training advanced, our weekly training changed. At the end of the second week, the instructors started dropping us in the ocean twenty miles from shore so that we could swim ashore. During my third ocean drop, I felt mischievous so I sprinted a short distance ahead of the main group. Normally, we would swim in groups of three. Swimming in small groups was a form of the buddy system. Each small group would stretch out in a line hanging on to one hand of the other swimmer(s) in the group. One member of the group would then kick and swim toward shore. Each member of the group would take a turn swimming and kicking. By alternating in this manner, the other members of the group were able to rest while one member of the group was swimming all the time. On this particular day, our instructors had dropped us off twenty miles from shore right after breakfast, and we had been swimming all day. We were getting closer to shore, and all of us were tired. Sometimes a little laughter or humor is just the right medicine to keep everyone going. To liven things up a bit, I decided to pull a prank. I hollered back to my buddies, "Hey, I have found an island." At this time, we were about a mile from shore. To pretend that I was standing on the island, I had started treading water. I had my body up to my waste out of the water. After I said that I had found an island, here my buddies came. When they got even with me, my buddies let down. I do not know how deep the water was there. They all went down blub, blub, blub! When they went down, I was laughing so hard that I almost choked on the salt water. When they came up spurting, they looked like sperm whales. From that point, the race was on for the Coronado Strand. The Coronado Strand was our nickname for the Coronado peninsula that was connected to California by a stretch of land called the Silver Strand. The Silver Strand beach was located approximately one mile from downtown San Diego, California. Today, the Coronado Strand is connected to the mainland by the Coronado-San Diego Bridge and can be accessed either by car or a short ferry ride from San Diego. The Silver Strand is now a State Beach in California, and it stretches south of Coronado for seven miles connecting with Imperial Beach.

I swam as hard as I could to escape the wrath of my buddies, but once we got on shore, they finally caught me. After catching me, my buddies hard-legged me. The term hard-legged was slang for punishing someone by using your knee to strike the offending person's thigh. When they finished, I barely could walk. That was the last time I pulled a prank like that on my buddies.

Another aspect of our training in the UDT was learning how to dive. Our diving instruction included learning how to dive in shallow as well as deep water. We also practiced setting explosive charges to sink ships and to salvage ships. When diving or swimming in cold water, we would coat our skin with grease to prevent a loss of body heat. Since most of our diving occurred off the coast of San Diego where the water is warm, we rarely used grease. However, around San Francisco, California or Seattle, Washington the water was cold, and you needed grease to prevent a loss of body heat. Losing body heat in cold water could send you into hypothermia, which could lead to mission failure and the loss of your life. The instructors made certain that all members of the UDT understood the dangers related to hypothermia.

The diving equipment used today has changed dramatically from what we used in the UDT. The breathing apparatus, which we used for shallow dives down to about 100 feet, consisted of an air recycling canister sealed inside a canvas bag. You blew up the two tubes of the canvas bag by hand on the surface. Air from the bags went through the recycling canister and through a tube back into the mask. To emphasize the care that we needed to take when wearing this canister, the instructors removed a canister from the canvas bag and threw it into a tub of salt water. When the canister hit the salt water, it exploded. The lesson from that demonstration was that you better not tear the canvas bag containing the canister. If you did, the canister would blow up like a stick of dynamite going off. Knowing how explosive the canister was when it came in contact with salt water made me very cautious when using this breathing apparatus. I certainly did not want to tear the canvas bag on the breathing apparatus while under water.

There are many people who have fantasized about what it is like to dive. They have seen movies where the water is crystal clear, and you can see the bottom. However, diving is very difficult requiring both discipline and physical stamina. One of the most important considerations for diving is water clarity. Clear water can make the dive site much safer. Conversely, the dive site can be a major disappointment when clouded by a veil of murky water, algae growth, or debris. Visibility under water is generally a measurement of the distance at which an object underwater can be readily identified. We measured underwater visibility in two ways: (1) horizontal visibility — how far you could see looking straight ahead, and (2) vertical visibility — how far you could see looking up or down. Of the two, we considered horizontal visibility the most important, since it affected our perception of the underwater environment and our ability to keep track of our dive buddies. In most places in the ocean, you cannot see farther than a couple of feet. In short, even divers with very powerful lights are required to feel around in the dark.

A critical part of our UDT training involved an intense period of instruction on the use of explosives. During this period of instruction, each of us were issued a utility belt to wear. This utility belt was very durable and suitable for many different types of pouch attachments. Some referred to this utility belt as a web belt. These web belts were adjustable for a comfortable fit and were available in a range of sizes to ensure a utility belt suitable for every member of our UDT class. Along with the utility belt, each of us was given a small pouch with a small bottle of nitro glycerin to attach to the utility belt. Like all good students, we took the utility belts, placed the pouch containing the nitro glycerin on the belt, and adjusted the belt to fit around our waist. After the first demonstration on how to use nitro glycerin, I felt unsafe wearing this utility belt. During this demonstration the instructor used nitro glycerin, a one pound ball-peen hammer, and a two hundred pound anvil. A ball-peen hammer has two ends, one ball-shaped and the other more cylindrical. There are variety of different ball-peen hammers, and today they may have a metal, fiberglass, or wooden handle. A ball-peen hammer is used primarily for both shaping and striking metal, including striking punches and chisels in metal fabrication. Before this demonstration, we were placed behind an eight inch thick layer of special glass which we could see through. Our instructor took an eye dropper and carefully placed a couple of drops of nitro glycerin on the anvil. After moving into a protective location, the instructor elevated the ball-peen hammer using a pulley system so that it was directly above the anvil. When the ball-peen hammer was dropped onto the anvil, it set off the nitro glycerin which disintegrated the ball-peen hammer and about half of the anvil. At the conclusion of this demonstration, I tried to give my bottle of nitro glycerin to my buddies, but none of them wanted it. I never liked using explosives, but there were men in my UDT class who could blow the rungs out of the chair you were sitting in and bet money that they could accomplish this without turning your chair over. Whenever we had any free time, these explosive junkies as I refer to them would be playing with their explosives. Because of their desire to try new explosive techniques, I hated to be in the same room with them when they were experimenting.

The hand to hand combat training, which we received in UDT was the best available at that time. One part of this hand to hand combat included using a pole which resembled a giant q-tip. This pole was approximately five feet long with rubber cushions on the ends about 6 inches in diameter, and it was known as a pugil stick. Historically, the pugil stick had been used since the early 1940s by military personnel in training for rifle and bayonet combat, and it is still used today by the United States military. Unlike the normal use of the pugil stick for rifle and bayonet training, our instructors wanted us to meet our opponent with the pugil stick on a log, which straddled a mud hole. The goal was to strike each other with the pugil sticks until one or both of us fell into the mud. This whole concept seemed bizarre to me. Who in their right mind would go out onto a log straddling a mud hole to fight someone?

The way our instructors set up the pugil stick phase of our training was simple. Each of us had to get up on the log against the Limey (Englishman) instructor. The term Limey refers to a British sailor. For our UDT class, there was a British exchange instructor from the British Royal Marines. The British Royal Marines are the Marine Corps and amphibious infantry of the Royal Navy. We nicknamed this British Royal Marine, the Limey instructor. This Limey instructor was good at everything. The problem with this Limey instructor was that he received great satisfaction from hurting people. During a practice session with the pugil sticks, the commander in charge of UDT training told us that no one in the UDT class could have liberty until someone knocked the Limey instructor off of the log using a pugil stick. Three of the best in UTD class got up on the log, and the Limey instructor knocked them off. When it came my turn, I did not want to get out there with the Limey instructor because I had seen what he had done to those before me. However, I was unorthodox in my use of the pugil stick. When I got out there with him, the second he looked off I gigged him just like you would a fish. I hit him so hard with that pole right in the chest that he flipped backwards off the log. I literally knocked the breath out of him. A second instructor who had been watching my bout asked me to demonstrate the technique that I had used against the Limey instructor. This second instructor also ended up in the mud!

After I knocked the Limey instructor off the log into the

mud, the commander of the UDT training gave the whole UDT unit weekend liberty (forty-eight hours). During this liberty, four of us from the UDT unit went to San Diego to see a movie. On our way back to Coronado, where we were billeted, we walked by a location called "The Little Red Barn." On the billboard for the night, it advertised Bob Wills and the Texas Playboys featuring Tommy Duncan on vocals. Just kidding the others, I told them my brother's name is Tom Duncan. One of the group suggested that I tell the door keeper about this. So, I went up to the door keeper and said, "My brother's name is Tom Duncan." He invited me to come with him so we all went inside. When the doorkeeper told Bob Wills that Tom Duncan's brother and friends were there, Mr. Wills told him to seat us by the food and when they finished their set, the band would join us. In the meantime, Mr. Wills said, "Help yourself to the food, have a few drinks, and enjoy the music." The four of us pigged out. We had not eaten since breakfast. On the buffet table, there was sliced ham, turkey, bologna, cheese, baked beans, potato chips, pitchers of beer, and lots of soft drinks. When the band finished playing, they put up their instruments, and they came over to our table. Bob Wills, still holding his fiddle, addressed the group, "Which one of you is Tommy Duncan's brother?" I spoke up without hesitation, "My brother's name is Tom Duncan." He started laughing and told us, "You are our guest at the Little Red Barn. Please stay as long as you like."

The primary focus of the hand to hand combat training in the UDT was to teach us ways to hit a man, which would stop him or kill him by using one blow. Our first period of training in regular hand to hand combat started on a Thursday. During this period of instruction, I was picked to be the guinea pig by the Limey instructor that I had knocked into the mud hole with the pugil stick. In my own mind, I knew that the Limey instructor had chosen me because he wanted to regain his prestige and to get revenge for what he felt was a stain on his honor. When

I stepped into the ring, he threw me, hit me, jumped up and down on me, and kicked me. Somehow I managed to survive the beating that the Limey instructor inflicted on me. After this first period of instruction, I was hurt and sore in places that I did not know existed. The Limey instructor had beaten me to a pulp.

After taking this beating, I knew that during our next period of instruction on hand to hand combat that the Limey instructor would again choose me to beat on. Luckily, our next period of instruction on hand to hand combat training was not scheduled until the following Thursday. I knew that I had to learn to protect myself, if that was possible, before our next period of instruction. Through the grapevine, I learned that the Young Men's Christian Association, commonly known as the YMCA, in San Diego was teaching a Judo class. Desperate for help, I went to the YMCA for instruction. After some dickering on the price, I arranged for a special, condensed class on hand to hand combat from the Judo instructor. I had no intention of letting that Limey instructor use me for a punching bag again. The YMCA instructor was able to teach me techniques to counter several of the holds and moves that the Limey instructor had used. In addition, the Judo instructor showed me how to go limp rather than rigid, how to step on the arch of the attacker's foot, and how to hit the attacker who grabbed me on the ears with the heals of my hands. Furthermore, I learned a couple of special throwing techniques, which I practiced for several hours.

The next week, as I expected, the Limey instructor selected me to demonstrate the hand to hand combat skills against him. I let the Limey instructor come to me. When he made his move, I tripped him up and threw him out of the ring. The Limey instructor landed on his back outside the ring. Because of the impact, his breath had been knocked out of him. As the Limey instructor climbed back into the ring, I could see a mixture of fear and amazement in his eyes. He could not believe that the individual whom he had been teaching and whom he had beat to a pulp the prior week had learned enough to counter his attack and throw him out of the ring.

After returning to the ring, other members of my unit started taunting him. This made the Limey instructor extremely angry. Suddenly, the Limey instructor lunged forward and grabbed me. When he grabbed me, I went limp. This allowed me to bring my knees up and bicycle him right out of the ring onto his back again. From that point, the bout was a stand off. The Limey instructor knew that I was serious and that I intended to hurt him if I could.

Looking back on this hand to hand combat training I can unequivocally state that our training was very good. Our instructors were there to instill us with knowledge so that we could successfully overcome any enemy, infiltrate enemy lines, and accomplish our mission. The Limey instructor certainly motivated me to become proficient in hand to hand combat.

Our final test before graduation from the UDT required us to tread water across San Diego Bay in uniform with a rifle. We marched right off the pier two abreast with our rifles over our heads. To cross San Diego Bay each of us had to tread water for about half a mile. When we reached the other side our weapons were inspected to see if we had gotten them wet.

To entertain the attendees at our UDT graduation ceremony, we were required to march off the main deck of the Aircraft Carrier USS Valley Forge. The USS Valley Forge was one of twenty-four Essex-class aircraft carriers built during and shortly after World War II for the United States Navy. It was the first United States Navy ship to bear the name, Valley Forge, in honor of the 1777–1778 winter encampment of General George Washington's Continental Army in Valley Forge. The USS Valley Forge was commissioned in November 1946, too late to serve in World War II, but saw extensive service in the Korean War. The decision to have us march off the main deck of the USS Valley Forge was made in large part to impress Admiral Arthur

William Radford, who was the Vice Chief of Naval Operations. Admiral Radford was doing a command visit of Task Force 38, which was part of Third Fleet. I think that marching off the main deck of the USS Valley Forge was about the hardest thing I ever had to force myself to do. I would estimate that the main deck of the USS Valley Forge was at least 90 feet above the water. For this ceremony on the USS Valley Forge, we were lined up 4 abreast. I was in the first row. During the briefing before going up to the main deck, we had been instructed on how to keep from breaking our necks. The life preserver that each of us was wearing had a strip of wood that came right under our chins. We were instructed that we had to hold this wooden strip out past our chins. If we struck the water from that great a distance with the wooden strip under our chins, it could snap our necks back causing them to break. In addition, we were cautioned not to enter the water except feet first.

As I went across the main deck that morning, I double timed for about three steps. Then I looked out of the corner of my eye to see if anyone was passing me, but everyone was right behind me. When I jumped over the side, I tried to keep my feet pointed toward the water. As I plummeted toward the water, one instant my feet were down. The next instant my head was down. I must have made 3 or 4 complete revolutions before I struck the water. Luckily, when I struck the water, my feet were down. After striking the water feet first, my body traveled in a half moon arch. I did not much more than get wet until I was back on top of the water.

Because the UDT program was unproven, there was not sufficient funding from the United States Navy. Rear Admiral James H. Doyle who sponsored our UDT class decided that drastic measures were needed to save the UDT program. To win support throughout the United States Navy, Rear Admiral Doyle came up with an ingenious solution. He made a bet with Admiral Radford who was opposed to additional funding for the UTD program. The wager by Rear Admiral Doyle was that the UDT would be able to commandeer a United States Navy destroyer while the destroyer was at sea within 30 days. If the UDT was successful, Admiral Radford agreed to support additional funding for the UDT. If the UDT failed, Rear Admiral Doyle promised to terminate his push for additional funding for the UDT.

Under this wager, Admiral Radford had the advantage of knowing the time frame when our UDT unit would try to take over one of the Navy destroyers. However, we had the advantage of knowing where we would strike. All seventeen members of our UDT class were dropped off in the water at thirty yard intervals across the channel running along side of Goat Island a few miles outside the harbor at San Diego, California. Each of us carried an automatic weapon, knife, utility belt, and a grappling hook with a rope. When the first destroyer started through the channel, we had been bobbing in the channel for about six hours. As the destroyer came by, we were ready and climbed aboard. Taking over this ship was really very easy. All we had to do was take out the conning tower. The conning tower of a ship is the armored pilot house normally located above the engine room. Once we controlled the conning tower, we dogged and secured all the hatches coming topside, and captured the stern and bow watch. With our seventeen UDT members, accomplishing this task was a snap. The destroyer crew below deck never knew that we had taken charge of the ship. Without knowing it, the engine room crew on the destroyer was working for us. Instructions we sent from the conning tower were followed without question by those in the engine room. To let everyone know that we had control of the ship, we turned the United States flag upside down. We brought the destroyer right into port. After our success, Admiral Radford went to bat to obtain additional funding for the UDT program.

Almost the whole first year that I was in the Navy, I was

training. What those in our UDT class did not realize until much later was that most sailors never did the training that we did. After graduating from UDT, Fisher and I were assigned to Rear Admiral Richard Byrd's expedition to the North Pole on the ship called the USS Askari. The USS Askari was one of thirty-nine Achelous-class landing craft repair ships built for the United States Navy during World War II. Askari was an Arabic word meaning soldier.

CHAPTER 5
ALASKA EXPEDITION

The assignment of Fisher and me to the Alaska Expedition came as an incredible surprise. The day after graduating from the UDT, Fisher and I were ferried out to the USS Askari at 2:00 A.M. in the morning. Fisher and I had been placed aboard the USS Askari without knowledge of what our mission would be. No one in the UTD knew what happened to us, and we had no idea where we were going. Since Fisher and I were not part of the permanent ship's company of the USS Askari, we were tasked with the most unpleasant jobs on the ship. For those who have not been in the United States Navy, it is hard to understand what that means. We were categorized as "for further assignment." Because we were not part of the ship's company, we did not get the same privileges as the rest of the ship's crew. In short, we were given tasks to do, which the ship's company did not want to do. As you would expect, these were the hardest tasks. Since this was the first time that Fisher and I really had been at sea, we welcomed the opportunity to see the vast Pacific Ocean that we had been swimming around the edge of during UDT training. So despite all the unpleasant tasks, which we were given, our spirits were not dampened. The USS Askari that Fisher and I were placed on "for further assignment" was a troop transport/landing craft repair ship and not Rear Admiral Byrd's flag ship.

I remember the first time that I was able to look off the main deck of the USS Askari. The North Pacific was very rough. The USS Askari would go over one ground swell and plow through the next. It just so happened that the instant I stepped out onto the main deck, the ship plunged into a ground swell. Luckily, I was hanging onto the handrail as the ship went under water. If I had not been holding onto the railing, I might have been swept over board. During the few seconds that the ship was underwater, I felt like I was on a roller coaster. After almost drowning on the main deck, I developed a new respect for the Pacific Ocean and the officers piloting our ship. Fisher and I learned from the crew that our destination was Point Barrow, Alaska, but the route that we took was by no means direct. Point Barrow is located at the northernmost point of Alaska, on the Arctic Ocean. It was named by Frederick W. Beechey, a British explorer, for the British geographer Sir John Barrow. Over the years, Point Barrow has been the object of many expeditions to the North Pole and has figured prominently in Arctic aviation. Travel to Point Barrow by ship is open for only two or three months a year. During our trip to Point Barrow, we cut through the edge of Canada and the tip of Alaska. I learned that we went through the coastal islands along the edge of Canada and Alaska to protect our ship from the savage Pacific storms and to make our sailing easier.

After several days of steaming, we finally arrived at Point Barrow. Upon reaching Point Barrow, Fisher and I were assigned to work as drivers for Rear Admiral Byrd. Fisher and I did not realize that we would be helping Admiral Byrd become a famous polar explorer by assisting him in his travel to the North Pole. As drivers, one day Fisher would drive for Admiral Byrd and his surveyor, and the next day I would drive. On the days that I was not the driver and vice versa for Fisher, it was the responsibility of the one not driving to dig out and clean-off the modified jeep that we used to carry Admiral Byrd.

The weather north of the Arctic Circle defies description. Some days it would snow right out of the clear blue. No clouds were necessary for several feet of snow to fall. When I think of all the obstacles facing our efforts to travel to the North Pole, the weather was at the top of the list. Each day brought with it new weather related problems to overcome. I remember one day that it started snowing around 4:00 A.M.. By 5:00 A.M., the snow had stopped, but the snow had changed to sleet. When we finished eating breakfast at 7:00 A.M., the sleet had stopped. Then a cold rain started to fall. This cold rain ended around 8:00 A.M., and the temperature began to plummet. By noon, the temperature was 30 below zero. The conditions outside the ship were treacherous. The snow, sleet, and rain, which had been a slushy mess, changed into a solid sheet of ice. Everything was covered with ice. After witnessing the weather on that day, I knew that making a mistake in this climate would result in serious injury through frostbite or death from hypothermia. Each member of the expedition had received special training on the dangers of frostbite. Frostbite occurs when tissues freeze, which can happen within five minutes or less when bare skin is exposed to temperatures that are thirty degrees or more below zero. The nose, ears, cheeks, fingers, and toes are most affected by frostbite. Protecting the lungs from freezing during outside activity in extreme temperatures was also a serious concern. When the air temperature dropped to thirty degrees or more below zero, we were required to wear the balaclava and a special face mask to keep the face warm, to cover the mouth and nose, and to protect against blowing snow. By wearing the balaclava and a special face mask, the outside air was warmed some before being breathed into the lungs. Because the weather north of the Arctic was scary cold, it heightened my concern about frostbite and other weather related injuries.

For protection from the cold, all personnel leaving the USS Askari were required to put on layer after layer of cold weather gear. On my days to drive, I had on so much clothing that if I had fallen down, I could not have gotten back up. I looked like a giant teddy bear. In my mind, the layers of clothing made me feel secure from the cold. I did not believe that I could get cold with all that clothing on. It was hard to believe that I put on so many layers of clothing. Upon my return from the outside, it took me about two hours to get undressed so that I could go to the bathroom. Proper clothing was not the only requirement for those leaving the ship. Every person leaving the ship was given a cup of hot whale oil to drink. The Eskimos of Alaska used whale oil for food and fuel. In fact, the Eskimos used every part of the whale in everyday life. Whale blubber was used for food, gum, and facial products; the vertebrae were used for seats, and the stomach and bladder were used for drums. Drinking whale oil was part of the daily routine for every Eskimo, but for me drinking whale oil was worse than drinking castor oil. The minute that I tasted whale oil I knew that the Eskimos had to be out of their minds. Whale oil was terrible, and it smelled like fermenting fish. Personally, I could not understand how anyone could drink whale oil voluntarily. After drinking whale oil, I re-evaluated my opinion of the Eskimos. Furthermore, it was hard for me to comprehend why anyone would choose to live in such a harsh environment surrounded by ice and extreme cold.

For all sailors leaving a United States Navy ship, there is a specific protocol to be followed. Before proceeding down the gangway, you must first request permission to leave the ship while saluting the Duty Officer. When permission has been granted by the Duty Officer, you turn to the stern of the ship and salute the United States Ensign (flag). After completing this protocol, you may debark. Standing with the Duty Officer on the USS Askari was the sailor responsible for issuing each departing sailor a cup of hot whale oil to drink. The Duty Officer at the gangway of the USS Askari had to be sharp to make sure that I drank my whale oil before debarking. If I could distract him and the issuing sailor, I would dump my whale oil over the side before they could blink their eyes. Normally, I would act as though I was tasting my whale oil. If the Duty Officer and the issuing sailor ever looked away, my whale oil was gone.

Being a skeptic, I was never certain that Admiral Byrd found the North Pole. The ice terrain that we encountered in the Arctic region is difficult to put into words. For me, being on all that ice was unnerving. In some ways, our trek across the Arctic was like going through a maze, and we were the rats. In places we were confronted by jagged ice standing up edgewise twenty to thirty feet high. Our means of transportation for this trek was a converted jeep. This converted jeep had two little skis on the front in place of the front wheels. The skis on the front were about two feet long and eight to ten inches wide. On the back, in place of wheels, were longer skis approximately eight feet in length and ten inches wide. The two shorter skis in the front were used for steering. If you were lucky, you could turn this contraption around in a football field. At the rear of the jeep for propulsion was an airplane engine with a propeller mounted on a tripod. This converted jeep looked a lot like the air boats you see today in the Florida Everglades. Fastened behind the propeller was a crude piece of sheet metal, which acted as a tail rudder. This rudder was supposed to direct the air from the propeller in the direction desired by the driver. Driving this converted jeep was an experience. At times, I could turn the short skis in the front, but they would have no effect on our direction of travel. In simple terms, this contraption was impossible to maneuver. If conditions were right, you could direct the air in the back, turn your front skis, and the contraption would go the way you wanted.

In our search for the North Pole, we encountered places where there were mounds of ice for miles in either direction with no way around them. Since these mounds were too steep for the jeep to go over, we had to bring in a demolition team to blow a hole through them. To mark our route, individuals following in our trace put up little flags. These flags marked our forward progress. Each day we would start up again where we left off by following the marker flags. The naval officer who was surveying our course never convinced me that he knew where we were or where we were going. We had several different kinds of compasses with us. For our expedition, magnetic compasses were not worth a plug nickel. The magnetic compass works because the Earth is like a giant magnet, surrounded by a huge magnetic field. The Earth has two magnetic poles which lie near the actual North and South Poles. Within the typical magnetic compass, the magnetic field of the Earth causes a magnetized needle of iron or steel to swing into a north-south position, which displays the direction of the horizontal component of the Earth's magnetic field at the point of observation. Since we were so close to the magnetic North Pole and the hulls of our steel ships, the magnetic compasses would not function properly. One minute the magnetic compass would point in one direction, and the next minute it would point in a different or opposite direction. However, the gyrocompasses worked very well. A gyrocompass is a type of non-magnetic compass, which is based on a fast-spinning disc and rotation of the Earth to automatically find geographical direction. Gyrocompasses are widely used for navigation because they have two significant advantages over magnetic compasses: (1) they find true north as determined by the Earth's rotation, which is different from, and navigationally more useful than, magnetic north, and (2) they are unaffected by ferromagnetic materials, such as a ship's steel hull.

Each day the surveyor would take out his sexton, take a couple of sightings, and try to figure out where we were. When the surveyor would talk, what he said did not make sense to me, but this may have been because I was concerned more about how we were going to get over the next ice obstacle in front of us. When no way could be found around an ice obstacle, we brought in the demolition team to set explosives in the ice wall to blow a hole large enough for the jeep to go through. Accompanying us on these daily excursions were dog teams with sleds. These dog teams were supposed to scout for routes through the ice. In my opinion, the dog teams were useless since the dogs went pretty much where they wanted. The day that Admiral Byrd finally reached the location that he called the North Pole, Fisher was driving. I never did get to see the so called North Pole.

After our search for the North Pole was complete, Fisher and I became involved in transporting a shipment of lumber to the top of Pyramid Mountain, which is located near the mouth of Kodiak Bay. The term Kodiak is a Russian word meaning "island" that came from the early Russian fur trappers who settled on this island in the 1790's. Kodiak Bay is located on the east side of Kodiak Island and just south and west of Kanai peninsula in the southern part of Alaska. Kodiak Island lies on the south coast of Alaska, separated from the Alaska mainland by the Shelikof Strait. After hauling the lumber to the top of this mountain, we built a target for the United States Air Force. The process that we went through to build this target is a good example of how ludicrous some of the decisions by our military commanders were. A week of hard work was required to get all the lumber up on top of this mountain. To get the lumber up the mountain, we had to use pulleys, cables, and brute physical strength. Once the lumber was on top of the mountain, we had to climb around on the ice to build the target. Upon completion of the target, an Air Force fighter flew by on one pass and blew it up. In my opinion, building the target on top of this mountain was an exercise in stupidity. What I did not understand was why we even needed the lumber. What we should have done was just paint a big bulls' eye on the ice and let the Air Force shoot at that, unless the ultimate goal was to let the Eskimos have the lumber which had been blown into kindling.

While I was in Alaska, I got to go into an Eskimo house (igloo). Personally, I do not think that igloos will ever become fashionable. The Marines on our ship even instructed us during cold weather survival training on how to build igloos. I watched the Marines cut out the blocks of snow and ice for an igloo. While I watched them, I thought to myself, "Staying warm in an ice house is ridiculous. There is no way that anyone could convince me that I would ever be warm in an igloo." In igloos, the walls are made of ice, the ceiling is made of ice, and the floor is made of ice. Skins covered the walls and floor, and a tallow bowl with a wick burned in the center of the igloo as a heater. Sitting in an igloo reminded me of being in a freezer. The Marines told me that the temperature would rise to almost sixty degrees inside the igloo. As part of our cold weather training, each of us was required to spend time in an igloo. When I crawled into the igloo, I had to stay hunched over or sit down because the igloo was not tall enough for me to stand up. In fact, igloos are not big enough to cuss a cat in without getting fur in your mouth. In addition to the psychological problem of dealing with an igloo being made of ice and snow, the air inside the igloo became polluted from the smoke from the tallow burning. Igloos do not have vents to let in fresh air. With the smoke from the whale oil burning, living in an igloo would be miserable. Furthermore, the wick burning the oil in the tallow bowl in an igloo was like having a candle burning in a room 9 feet in diameter. These facts convinced me that an igloo was a last resort for survival.

While North of the Arctic Circle, the USS Askari held a special ceremony in accordance with United States Navy tradition for becoming a Blue Nose. To become a Blue Nose a sailor only needed to be on board a Navy ship that crossed the Arctic Circle. The Blue Nose ceremony varies based upon the crew of the ship conducting the ceremony. On the USS Askari, most of the crew to include Fisher and I were declared to be non-blue nose slugs. As non-blue nose slugs, we were required to run around in circles on the main deck in our skivvies staring at the Aurora Borealis. Next, buckets of seawater were thrown on us while we stared at the Aurora Borealis. Finally, our noses were painted blue with watercolor paint, and a service record book entry of the date and time of our crossing the Arctic Circle was made.

Just prior to our departure from Alaska to return to Seattle, Washington, some of the sailors on the USS Askari got into big trouble when they took a totem pole from an Eskimo village. These sailors had tied the totem pole on the front of the USS Askari. This totem pole had several ugly faces carved into it. To the local Eskimos, this totem pole had cultural, religious, and historical importance. Even before the totem pole incident most of the Eskimos disliked Americans, but after the sailors on our ship stole the totem pole, the Eskimos became hostile. To win back the trust and cooperation of the Eskimos for the United States' presence in Alaska, the United States Navy established a program to give away a rifle called the 222 Hornet. From personal shooting experience, I found the 222 Hornet to be one of the best rifles that was ever made. This splendid weapon was ideal for hunters like the Eskimos. The shell of a 222 Hornet has the same amount of lead as a normal 22 caliber, but the 222 shell contained as much powder proportionately as a 30-30 shell. Small game could be taken with the light load 222 shell while larger game could be brought down with the high end load 222 shell. What I liked about the 222 Hornet was that the projectile would have already hit and passed through the target before the report of the rifle. This weapon was excellent for shooting caribou, which travel in herds. A good shot could shoot several caribou before the herd knew what was happening and got spooked by the rifle report. We gave every Eskimo male over the age of eighteen a 222 Hornet and a box of shells.

Looking back on this program, I feel that it was an expensive method for the United States government to use to win the acceptance of the Eskimos. Some might even view this rifle give away program as a bribe. One day, I was assigned the duty to stand out in the cold to hand out these weapons. My orders were that only male Eskimos over the age of eighteen were to receive a free weapon and a box of shells. The problem was how do you tell the women from the men? Men could not be distinguished from women by their faces since all Eskimos look alike when they are all dressed up in their cold weather clothes. When the Eskimos came to my distribution point for their weapon, I would ask them if they were a man or woman. Their answer would be "Ugh!" So I would have them sign the paperwork and give them a rifle and a box of shells. The temperature outside while I was giving out these rifles was around 30 degrees below zero. Fisher and I really enjoyed distributing these weapons. As part of the cold weather gear, we were required to wear shaded goggles. Wearing these goggles hampered the weapon distribution because it distorted our vision. Furthermore, I barely could write because of the gloves on my hands. When I came back on board the ship, the Senior Chief Petty Officer asked, "How many weapons did you give away?" I replied, "How many signed papers do I have?" Looking at the papers, he said, "Who is this? I can't read this name." I stated, "I don't know because they did not bring me their birth certificate before they signed the paperwork."

As luck would have it, the Marines on our ship were tasked to teach the Eskimos how to shoot. Can you imagine teaching a group of Eskimos who cannot speak English and who were still using whale bones as weapons how to shoot? As part of this training process, I was also required to show the Eskimos how to shoot. There was a herd of caribou about twelve hundred yards away. One of the Eskimos who could speak English said, "You shoot caribou." Then he pointed to the herd of caribou. I opened the sites on that 222 Hornet as far as they would go. Next, I adjusted the sites for what I considered the approximate windage. The top range for the site on the 222 Hornet was about twelve hundred yards. This worked out perfect because that was about how far away the herd was. It was just a lucky guess on my part as to distance. In Alaska, distance is difficult to calculate because of the vast flat lands and open spaces. Distance is much easier to determine when there are mountains or terrain changes to break up the flat land.

The Eskimos that I taught how to shoot wanted me to stay and hunt for them. With that 222 Hornet, I shot four caribou. When I sighted in the rifle, I brought it to my shoulder and rotated the rifle from left to right bringing the sights into view. As the sights came up and crossed the lead caribou in the herd, I fired. My firing of the weapon was made in one fluid motion. Almost as soon as I pulled the trigger, the caribou fell dead. Before the rifle report could be heard by the remaining caribou, I shot three more. The Eskimos that I showed how to shoot thought that the way I rotated the rifle from left to right had something to do with making the bullet hit the caribou. When I handed the rifle to the first Eskimo, he tried to imitate my actions in firing the weapon. His imitation included the rotation of the weapon from left to right. It was not until I saw the Eskimo trying to imitate me that I realized what I had done. I guess the rotation motion, which brought the sights up was just an old habit that I had picked up as a young boy in Tennessee. I always was accused of firing too fast. In boot camp the range instructor would tell me that I did not take my time, but the truth is I get bored if I try to take a lot of time when firing a weapon. Some people are just naturals, or they have what is called fast eyes. I probably had about the fastest eyes of anyone. When I joined the Navy in 1948, I had 20/10 vision. I could see the stitching and the word Spalding written on a baseball when it was thrown. The truth is that I really could see. This also was true when I was shooting. When I was on the range, I never had to have anyone wave Maggie's Drawers at me. I knew where the weapon hit because I could see where the bullet hit the target. Few men had hands and eyes as well coordinated as mine.

While in Alaska, the sailors on the ship that I was on were given Liberty to go hunting by the Captain. Before leaving the ship, we were briefed to avoid shooting bears because they were very dangerous when wounded. An hour after leaving the ship a friend of mine named Weaver shot a Kodiak Bear. As soon as he shot the bear, Weaver came running as fast as he could to where I was hunting. There were three other sailors with me when Weaver came running up. I had killed a moose which weighed about 1500 pounds, and the three of us were trying to load it onto the jeep. As Weaver came running up to me, he said, "Red, I just shot a bear and he's coming!" Sure enough, I looked over Weaver's shoulder, and there the bear was coming at us for all he was worth. Picking up my M-1 rifle, which had a seven shot clip, I threw it into my shoulder, and I put all seven shots in the head of that Kodiak Bear as he was running toward me. The bear did not fall until he was about forty-five feet from me. You talk about doing some serious shooting! I was doing my best to stop that bear. I was frightened, because if I did not stop the bear, we were in trouble. There was no way we could outrun a bear. Depending on the type of bear, they can run from twenty to thirty miles per hour while the world class speed for man is about fifteen miles per hour. Later, as we looked at that Kodiak bear, his head was mush. The problem with shooting a bear in the head is that bears do not have a very large brain. But there was no doubt about this Kodiak Bear having an air-cooled brain after I fired seven shots through his head.

When we got back to the ship with all our game, the ship's cook tried to feed that bear to us. The ship's cook was a sailor named Fields from Georgia. He was the best at cooking wild meat, but he never did fix that bear where it was fit to eat. When meat from that bear was cooking, it smelled like a wet dog. Fields was great at cooking other types of wild meat such as wild ducks, deer, and caribou. To take the mud-like taste out of the wild ducks, Fields would place small, peeled onions in the duck's cavity while it was cooking. Somehow the onions would absorb and remove the mud-like taste from the duck. I assumed that the onions did this by absorbing the fluids that cooked out of the duck's cavity while simultaneously flavoring the duck with onion.

From start to finish, our efforts to locate the North Pole and afterward our adventures in Alaska took a little over two and a half months. Surprisingly, Fisher and I found ourselves back in the continental United States at Seattle, Washington, in March of 1949. Years later, after I had gotten out of the Navy, Admiral Byrd returned to the North Pole. I still have the newspaper clipping about Admiral Byrd's return trip to the North Pole to find his storage cave containing the lanterns, biscuits, and other things that he left during our expedition to the North Pole.

CHAPTER 6
TRIP TO THE FAR EAST

On our return route from the expedition to the North Pole, the USS Askari that Fisher and I were on made a port call in Juneau, Alaska. The USS Askari was the first United States Navy ship that had made a port call in Juneau since the 1930's. While we were in Juneau, Admiral Byrd's flag ship arrived, and he made a big speech to all the sailors about granting them leave when we got back to Seattle, Washington. Before leaving Juneau, Alaska, I wrote home to my mother that I would be coming home on leave because Admiral Byrd had promised that each sailor would receive up to 30 days leave if he had that much on the books. All the sailors on the USS Askari were excited upon our arrival in Seattle. We felt like conquering heroes because of the successful expedition to the North Pole. I expected to receive thirty days leave upon docking in Seattle since I had that much time on the books. Admiral Byrd had promised this leave as a reward for the harsh conditions that we endured on the expedition to the North Pole.

To my surprise, the day that the USS Askari docked in Seattle, I was placed on another naval vessel, the USS Achernar AKA 53, headed for Shanghai, China. I will remember that day as long as I live. My transfer to the USS Achernar occurred at

7:00 P.M. on the 1st of March, 1949. Reassigned along with me was Fisher. Fisher and I seemed to be inseparable as we were together in boot camp, engineering school, yard certification training, UDT training, the expedition to the North Pole with Admiral Byrd, and now on a ship headed for Shanghai. From my perspective, it seemed like the United States Navy did not know what to do with us. All the other sailors who had graduated from the UDT had been assigned to a permanent command straight from school except for Fisher and me.

Three sailors, in addition to Fisher and me, were transferred to the USS Achernar as deck hands. For fifteen days after leaving Seattle, Washington, we rubbed the main deck of the AKA with what was called a honing stone. A honing stone is a stone fastened to a stick used to clean the deck of a ship. The surface of the main deck of this AKA was covered with two by fours to protect the steel deck from the cargo and containers. Every morning we would hone the main deck from 8:00 A.M. until 11:30 A.M. At 11:30 A.M., we would break for lunch. After the lunch break, we would resume honing the main deck until 4:30 P.M. I joked with the other deck hands that the purpose for honing was to build up our arm muscles.

Even now after over sixty years, I still do not understood what the purpose was for honing the main deck of the USS Achernar AKA 53. For me and the other sailors in the deck crew who had to hone the main deck day after day, morale was low. Being idealistic, I thought that there must be an important goal, which the Commander was trying to accomplish by this honing, but there was none. My physical effort and the efforts of the rest of the deck crew were without purpose or explanation. In sum, the monotonous honing of the main deck almost drove us crazy. Perhaps, if the Commander of the AKA had explained to us the purpose for the honing, we would have been able to accept this mindless work much easier. After honing the main deck from Seattle to Shanghai, it was as smooth as glass. To my fellow deck hands, I facetiously explained, "The main deck had to be as smooth as glass so that any sailor caught walking on the main deck during rough seas would slide overboard."

When we arrived in Shanghai, the Commander of the USS Achernar gave Fisher and me the opportunity to either sign up to sail on his ship or to work ashore at Shanghai. I did not have to think twice about whether I was going to work ashore or sign up to hone the deck of that AKA. Once I was assigned to shore duty, my new Commander gave me liberty. Prior to going on liberty, I wrote a letter to explain to my family that I would not be coming home to Perry County, Tennessee, on liberty because I was in Shanghai.

Liberty in Shanghai was a mistake. I had wanted to go on liberty to see some Chinese people because I had never seen a Chinese person. As I left the make shift Shanghai naval base on liberty, the first thing that I saw was a small rock bridge. This rock bridge was made of stone without any cement or concrete. The stream under this rock bridge was nothing more than a sewage drain off into the East China Sea from Shanghai. Raw sewage poured into this stream from the gutters of every Shanghai street along its path. The stench from this small stream almost knocked me down. Braving the stench, I continued up the street. I tried to hold my breath as I ran the next hundred yards. My objective was to put as much distance as possible between me and that stream as quickly as I could. Suddenly, I came to a stop about three blocks from that stream because laying on the edge of the road in the gutter was a little baby. The baby was about six months old. Covering this baby were hundreds of flies. The baby was almost black because of the flies all over him. Flies were in his eyes, in his mouth, and in his ears. The skin on the baby was swollen so tight that it looked like it would explode if it were stuck with a pin. My nostrils became filled with the smell of this baby's rotting flesh. This dead baby was quite a shock to me and my upbringing. I was raised in rural Tennessee. The morals of the society, which I was raised in, dictated that you would take dead bodies and bury them. You did not leave the dead bodies right on the side of the road for everyone to see.

After seeing this dead baby, my stomach started to do flip flops. In an effort to avoid vomiting right on the spot, I turned away from the dead baby holding my nose with one hand and placing my other hand over my mouth. Tears brimmed up in my eyes as an overwhelming urge to flee struck me. I closed my eyes and blindly started running up the road. After a few steps, I opened my eyes, but the tears made everything blurry. When my eyes finally cleared, I was a couple of blocks further up the street. As I came around a bend in the street, I saw an old Chinese man laying in the road. The old Chinese man was on his side with his feet facing my direction of approach. The head of the old Chinese man was turned sideways toward the gutter. As the sunlight hit the side of this old man's face, I could see that he had a beard and weathered features. I really could not tell how old he was. His brown skin looked rough and leathery. Only by long hours of toiling in the sun could someone's skin become so leathery and calloused. Feeling that this old Chinese man was in need of help, I swiftly moved toward him, reached down, and turned him over by his shoulder. From this touch, I could tell that his body was semi-stiff from the start of rigor mortis. Rigor mortis is a stiffening effect of the body after death. As the body of the old Chinese man rolled over, the other side of his head came into view. I jumped back in horror because the whole side of this old man's head was eaten up. Maggots were working alive in and out of the side of his head. I had never seen as many maggots and blow flies as there were on the side of this old man's head. When I saw this, my stomach turned inside out. Quickly, I moved to the side of the street where I vomited. Once my gagging stopped, the only thought on my mind was getting back to base as fast as possible. Never before had I seen such filth and total disregard for human life. As I crossed over the rock bridge on my return, I saw the Enlisted Men's Club. When I saw the Enlisted Men's Club, I sprinted straight for it. A big Marine Sergeant was running the club. That Marine Sergeant took one look at me and said, "If I ever saw a man who needed a drink, you need one." He reached under the bar and got a fifth of whiskey, poured me a shot, and left the bottle. I sat right there until I had drunk that fifth of whiskey. From then on, I never tried to go ashore or off base in Asia without first having a couple of drinks. This was the only way I could stand going on liberty in the Far East.

Of all the Asian countries, China was the most filthy. Japan on the other hand was relatively clean. Unlike China, the Japanese took great pride in their cleanliness. For example, in China it was not uncommon for a man or woman to stop right in front of you or on the side of the road and go to the bathroom. Many times only my quick reflexes prevented me from walking into them. Also, in China it was extremely important to watch where you walked, or you might step in earlier deposited bowel movements on the road.

Another surprise to me was the fact that there were Chinese individuals whose job was to collect bowel movements to put on their gardens and rice fields. These individuals were known as honey dippers. The honey dippers collected the human waste that drained into each town square through a series of benjo ditches. The benjo ditches collected human waste from the Chinese dwellings and homes located along each side of the benjo ditch and carried it downgrade to the central pool in the town square. The central pool, where the human waste collected, looked like a stone lined pit about eight feet deep. The honey dippers would come along and dip out the human waste and place it in containers sitting on a horse drawn cart. This horse drawn cart was known as the honey wagon. By way of the honey wagon, the containers with the human waste would be transported to the local agricultural fields. Near these fields, the containers from the honey cart would be emptied into a large pit. The human waste was supposed to remain in this pit to go through further fermentation and decay until it could be spread as fertilizer. When a honey dipper was transporting this human excrement, the aroma, which preceded him, was like a steam roller. One day on liberty in downtown Shanghai, I quite by accident observed a honey dipper at work. The honey dipper had a little cart with two buckets. At first, I did not know what he was doing. Luckily, I was down wind or the smell would have ended my curiosity. From the rise in the street where I stood, I could see this honey dipper climbing in and out of what looked like a large circular stone well in the center of a large intersection. As I drew closer, I could see that he was dumping the buckets, which he filled from the well into his cart. After dumping the buckets, he would climb back down into the well. Not until I ventured within about twenty feet did the smell hit me. What I thought was a well, turned out to be a community bathroom. Chinese living around this intersection would squat on the stone rim of this well structure to go to the bathroom. The Chinese sitting around the top of this well structure reminded me of quail sitting on a roost. On the roads around the rice fields in Shanghai, I have seen honey dippers with yokes over their shoulders and a bucket on either side. In these buckets, they carried human waste. If you were not careful as the honey dipper past you on the road, he might brush you with a bucket or splash some of the human excrement on you as you passed.

Operating out of Shanghai was the United States Navy's largest salvage unit. This salvage unit was part of a massive effort to clean up ship wreckages, which littered the Pacific in the aftermath of World War II. After being in Shanghai for about two weeks, I read a special United States Navy notice on the White Hat's Bulletin Board. According to this notice, there soon would be a fifth salvage crew, and volunteers were needed to man this new crew. Some of the sailors around me commented that joining a salvage crew was like joining a suicide crew. The stereotype of a salvage crew was that the sailors assigned to it had a short lifespan because of accidents and drowning. I said to myself, "Anything would beat staying in Shanghai." So, I signed up to join the salvage crew. Later, that same day, I ran into Fisher. Fisher asked, "Are you going to sign up for the salvage crew?" I responded, "I already have." Fisher replied, "I'm going to sign up and get out of this place too!" With our UDT background, Fisher and I did not have any problem getting assigned to the new salvage unit. In fact, the Salvage Unit Commander was elated to have sailors with our background. For the next three months, I worked in a salvage crew. Salvage was work that came natural to me. Soon, I practically was running the salvage team to which I had been assigned.

My opportunity for advancement in the salvage community came when a First Class Petty Officer by the name of Galt from Alabama who was the crew leader on a sister salvage crew decided to retire from the Navy. Galt had twenty-eight years in the Navy, and the Salvage Unit Commander was looking for somebody to replace him. From my perspective, the main qualifications for salvage crew leader were: (1) that you had to have an excellent knowledge of the Bible; (2) that you had to be a historian and know more about the United States Civil War than anyone else in the salvage crew; and (3) that you had to be able to whip any man in the outfit. The third qualification was most important because on a salvage mission you must depend on yourself and your crew since there is no one else present to help. In other words, a salvage crew had to be self sufficient and independent. Everyone had to pull his fair share of the load. Members of the salvage crew learned to rely on one another as a team. Normally, the salvage crew and its gear would be left behind on a small boat or dropped off by the Mother ship on an uncharted island near the ship wreckage that was to be salvaged. Ultimately, it was you, God Almighty, the sharks, and survival of the fittest.

Because being a salvage crew leader was such a difficult job, the Salvage Unit Commander was hesitant to put me in charge of Galt's salvage crew. The primary problem from the Commander's perspective was my age. I was just barely eighteen. Finally, the Commander decided to test me. So he put me in charge of the salvage crew on a small island where two ships were lodged off shore in the mud under about fifty feet of water. To the amazement of the Commander, I quickly and efficiently salvaged both ships. My leadership skills so impressed the Salvage Unit Commander that I became his top salvage crew leader. My reputation as a salvage crew leader became infamous. Whenever the Salvage Unit Commander wanted a tough, mean crew, he selected mine.

The United States Navy always stressed the importance of the buddy system when going on liberty in a foreign country. Under the buddy system, naval personnel should never go on liberty alone. This point became crystal clear to me during the second liberty that I took in Shanghai. My salvage crew and I had just returned from a long salvage operation. Because of increased unrest in China, the Navy had put together a special brief on how to deal with Chinese gangs. During this brief, I was informed that the Chinese sometimes attacked western European and American sailors in large groups. The Chinese would not attack one on one, but came in bunches, like bananas. After receiving this brief, I went back to my salvage crew, and I briefed them. The next day, five of my salvage crew (including me) decided to go on liberty in Shanghai. On our return, as we were walking back to the base, we heard wooden shoes all around us. There must have been one hundred or more Chinese following us. The briefer had said, "To frighten the gang, grab one of the Chinese gang members and make him scream in pain." All of a sudden, the Chinese surrounded us. They were using broom handles to beat us. I grabbed the first Chinese gang member who got close to me, and I straightened his arm out. As I straightened his arm out, I brought it down across my knee until it popped like a dry corncob. Instead of screaming in pain, the Chinese gang member fainted in my arms. By now, we were literally being beaten to death. I grabbed a broom handle before it struck me in the head. My hands stopped the blow, but it stung my hands. Once I had my hands on the broom handle, I jerked real hard. This caused the Chinese gang member who tried to hit me to lose his balance. As this gang member fell toward me, I grabbed him. I put one hand on his collar bone and the other hand on his jaw. It was my goal to make him scream. When I got my fingers dug in under his collar bone, this Chinese gang member let out a blood curdling scream. As briefed, this scream worked. It frightened the other Chinese gang members, and they fled. I was extremely happy to hear the sound of all those wooden shoes running down the street away from us. All it took was one scream! When the Chinese had cleared out, Barringer turned to me and said, "I would never have thought of pulling their heads off." We had a good laugh about that.

My salvage crew had the reputation of being the toughest and most efficient in the United States Navy. In fact, my salvage crew salvaged and sailed one ship that was broken completely in half. The Lieutenant who assigned this salvage mission to me thought that this wreckage would be impossible to salvage. In fact, he had planned to use this mission to soil my reputation in the salvage community. His deceit instead resulted in his court-martial because I did exactly what he ordered, which was to bring the salvaged ship into Pearl Harbor, Hawaii. As we started into Pearl Harbor with this salvaged ship, the harbor master almost had a fit. We brought this ship in with the stern engines running, towing the bow of the ship which was bobbing along in trace. The harbor master said to me, "You can't bring that ship in here." I looked at him and said, "I have been ordered to bring this ship into the harbor." I reached into my pocket, pulled out my orders, and showed them to him. The harbor master did not know what to do. While the harbor master went off to contact the United States Navy about this matter, my crew brought the salvaged ship into the harbor in two halves and put it into the naval yards for repair. After putting both halves in the naval yards, the repairmen were able to splice it back together. My salvage crew helped the yard crew line up the two halves so that they could make the splice. Bringing in this ship in two halves was very dangerous because either half could have sunk with my salvage crew on board. Furthermore, if the two halves of this salvaged ship had sunk in Pearl Harbor, access in and out of the harbor might have been blocked or restricted. In my own mind, I felt that sailing the two halves of this salvaged ship was no more dangerous than anything else that we did in salvage. The Lieutenant was court-martialed because he failed to follow proper procedures by ordering me to bring this ship into Pearl Harbor. In addition, the circumstances around this matter showed a clear lack of judgment on his part.

Only about half of my work in salvage took place while I was assigned to the make shift naval base in Shanghai. During this time period, bases in Taiwan were nonexistent and the bases in Japan were too far away from the ships, which needed to be salvaged. The British at this time controlled the port of Shanghai although much of the rest of China was in a state of turmoil. One night after celebrating a difficult salvage operation, my salvage crew and I were arrested for fighting by the British military police in Shanghai. The British military police mistakenly believed that they could hold us in a bamboo building. After examining the building, two of my crew kicked down the door, and we left the building.

With increased unrest brewing in China, my salvage crew and I were ordered to the Republic of the Philippines. We were placed on a Navy ship as part of a detachment, which was not a permanent part of the ship's company. In short, being a salvage crew placed us in the position of not having a ship we could call our own. We were just temporarily assigned to this ship for the ride down to the Philippines. Right after World War II in 1947, the United States leased from the Philippines two military bases, Clark Air Force Base and the United States Naval Base at Subic Bay. The job of my salvage crew was to help with the postwar reconstruction by salvaging ships that hampered access to Subic Bay. At this time, the United States was also trying to develop stronger ties with the Philippines and was working on a Mutual Defense Treaty, which ultimately was signed between the Philippines and the United States in 1951. After completing the salvage of two ship wreckages in the Philippines, my salvage crew and I were ordered back to mainland Japan for further salvage missions. For the salvage work along the coast of China and the Philippines, my salvage team and I were awarded a ribbon for China service and a ribbon for liberating the Philippines.

To get back to mainland Japan, my salvage crew and I were temporarily assigned to another Navy ship. A typhoon hit just as this Navy ship was ready to leave the Philippines. This typhoon had incredible wind speeds. Ultimately, it pushed the Navy ship we were on into the Indian Ocean. When the typhoon struck, this Navy ship was tied to the dock in Subic Bay. The Commander of the Navy ship tried to prevent the ship from being blown out to sea by the typhoon. Two ropes called hawsers secured the Navy ship to the dock. A hawser is a rope six inches in diameter. As the typhoon strengthened, the Navy ship was pushed out until the hawsers were taut. The winds and the rain continued to increase and intensify. At this point, the Commander of the Navy ship ordered the ship's engines to run at full speed toward the shore. Even with the engines running at full speed toward the shore, the ship continued to be blown toward the open sea. Suddenly, one of the hawsers snapped. With only one hawser holding the ship, there was great danger that the ship would be swamped and sunk while tied to the dock. If for some reason the ship were to turn parallel to the breakers, the ship would easily capsize and sink. Because of the danger of sinking, the Commander ordered the deck crew of the Navy ship to take fire axes and cut the remaining hawser. In the attempt to cut the remaining hawser, three men were washed overboard and lost. They were presumed to be dead.

Duty in Southeast Asia was much better once we went to mainland Japan. Being on mainland Japan was like returning to civilization after being in Shanghai and the Philippines.

CHAPTER 7
ATTEMPTED CHINESE BOARDING

W hen I arrived in Shanghai, China, in 1949, the political infrastructure of China was crumbling. A backlash of hatred for Europeans and Americans was sweeping across the country. This hatred for foreigners strengthened the Chinese Communist Party which was waging a civil war against the Chinese establishment, supported Chiang Kai-shek. Chiang Kai-shek was one of the most important political leaders in Chinese history, serving between Sun Yat-sen and Mao Tse-tung. He was the military and political leader who assumed leadership of the Kuomintang after the death of Sun Yat-sen in 1925. He commanded the Northern Expedition to unify China against the warlords and emerged victorious in 1928, as the overall leader of the Republic of China. Chiang led China in the Second Sino-Japanese War, which led to his international prominence. During the Chinese Civil War from 1927–1949, Chiang attempted to defeat the Chinese Communist Party forces, but he failed. This failure ultimately resulted in his retreat to Taiwan (Formosa) where he continued serving as the President of the Republic for the remainder of his life. In 1949, when the Communists forced Chiang Kai-shek to leave mainland China for Formosa, Formosa was nothing more than a mudflat island.

To those of us conducting salvage operations in southeast Asia, a safe place for resupply was critical. As long as the British, who were politically aligned with Chiang, maintained a naval base in Shanghai, United States Navy ships would have a safe location for resupply. On a normal salvage operation, my salvage team would travel from Shanghai to the salvage wreckage, complete the salvage mission, and return to Shanghai for resupply. Then we would turn around and do the same thing again.

As with all great upheavals in a society, the banner for change is usually carried by the younger generation. This was true for China. Chinese students supporting the Communist ideology set out to force all Europeans and Americans out of China. Because the port of Shanghai contained a large British naval presence, it became a prime target for protest by the Chinese Communist students and radicals.

As luck would have it, the United States Navy ship that my salvage team was attached to happened to be docked at the British pier in Shanghai for resupply when a large number of Chinese Communist students came down to protest. Everyone on our ship knew about the Chinese radicals who came down on the pier to protest the English presence two days earlier. As part of this protest, these Chinese Communist students had boarded an English (Limey) ship in port. So many Chinese forced their way on board that the ship sank right in the harbor. When our ship's crew saw a huge number of Chinese approaching our ship, we all assumed that the goal of these Chinese Communist students was the same as those who had sunk the Limey ship a couple of days earlier. However, as these Chinese students were soon to find out, selecting our ship to board was a major mistake. My salvage crew and the sailors who I worked with on the United States Navy ship that we were attached to were mean, tough, and fearless. We did not take abuse from anyone.

The Duty Officer on the gangway had already ordered a detachment of ten Marines from our ship to prevent the Chinese protestors from boarding our ship and to get them off the pier. The Marines were trying to make the Chinese leave the pier in accordance with their training. The rules that the Marines were following restricted the use of the billy club. The billy club is primarily a nonlethal defensive weapon when wielded appropriately. Historically, the billy club was made of wood, was no longer than the length of a person's arm, and was used to strike, ward off blows, aid in defensive maneuvers and holds, or simply to threaten escalated aggression. The billy club is not meant to deal lethal blows, and the military and police organizations that employ it specifically train their personnel not to strike the head or other vital areas of the human body, which could lead to death. Under those rules, you did not strike a person above the knees or around the head with the billy club. In addition, the Marines were trying to discourage the Chinese Communist students from advancing on the pier by spraying them with water from fire hoses. With about ten thousand Chinese trying to get on the pier and board our ship, the Marines were getting the tar beat out of them. These Chinese students were throwing rocks, bottles, and physically striking the Marines with clubs, broom handles, ax handles, and other farm hand tools. For Fisher, Barringer, and me, it was like watching a "Cowboy and Indian" movie. The Marines were like the "Cowboys" and the Chinese Communist students were like the "Indians." We were having a great time watching the action from up on the fan tail of the ship. We were screaming, hollering, and rooting for the Marines. Just as we started laughing at the Marines, the Captain of our ship came up. Our laughter infuriated the Captain so he told us, "You think it's so funny, you get down there. Stop the Chinese and clear the pier." After receiving this order, Fisher, Barringer, and I went down to the ship's armory, and each of us was issued a billy club about 30 inches long, which had a little leather loop on the end to put around our wrist. When Fisher, Barringer, and I went down the gangway of the ship to the pier, we were not concerned like the Marines about where we would hit the Chinese. When the three of us walked out on the pier, the Marines went back on board the ship. At this time, the Chinese Communist students thought they had us. The three of us spaced ourselves out to cover the pier, and the Chinese rapidly moved toward us. One of the Chinese students ran up and solidly hit me with a broom handle on the side of my head. The Chinese students were also hitting Fisher and Barringer. Because the Chinese students attacked us so aggressively with sticks and clubs, our fear turned into anger. There is nothing like being struck by a club or stick to fire one up. Once that student struck me in the head, my adrenalin started flowing, and I channeled my energy into clearing the pier. All three of us started functioning like a well oiled machine. Every time one of us swung our billy club, we hit about three or four Chinese students in the head. At first our progress was slow, but it was not long till the Chinese were jumping off that pier into the water. The Chinese who were facing us were backing over each other trying to get away. At the same time, the Chinese in the rear were pushing to get onto the pier. Our forward movement put the Chinese in the front of the mob in an untenable position. There was no place for them to go. Large numbers of them started jumping off the pier just to get away from us. When we swung our billy clubs, it was like cutting weeds with a sickle, and unlike the Marines, we never tried to hit anyone below the head. After hitting a Chinese student, if he was able to move at all, he got off the pier. In about an hour, we had the pier cleared. Several hundred injured Chinese students were being carried by their fellow Chinese students as fast as they could run.

Later, we learned that Chinese diplomats tried to make a big deal out of the way that we cleared the pier. When questioned about clearing the pier, we restated our orders, which were to stop the Chinese and to clear the pier. The Chinese got upset because several hundred of the Chinese students had serious injuries after we cleared the pier. What everyone seemed to overlook was that if we had not stopped the Chinese students and cleared the pier, they would have sunk our ship right in the harbor just as they had the Limey ship. In addition, the Chinese students were doing their best to hit us in the head with clubs, broom handles, ax handles, and other farm hand tools. In fact, many of the Chinese students were carrying stones and bottles, which they threw at us. After we cleared the pier, future United States Navy ships docked in Shanghai faced no further protests from the Chinese students.

The detachment of Marines that had been sent out to clear the pier had been trying to clear the pier without hurting the Chinese. The Marines were afraid to hit the Chinese students because they were afraid of getting into trouble. Likewise, when the Marines tried to spray them down with fire hoses, they decided not to use high pressure. If the Marines had put about one hundred pounds of pressure on the hoses, they would have been able to clear the pier by literally blowing the Chinese off the pier. The Chinese students sunk the Limey ship because they knew that they could get away with it. But after we cleared the pier that day, the Chinese Communist students knew better than to try to sink a United States Navy ship.

CHAPTER 8
WEST PAC

B y the end of 1949, the Chinese Communists finally forced the British to leave Shanghai. This in turn limited the ability of the United States Navy to conduct salvage operations in southeast Asia since there was no place for reliable resupply. As a result, the Salvage Unit Commander was ordered to move operations back to Hawaii. I was looking forward to getting back to Hawaii, since I had over forty days of leave on the books. With the planned movement back to Hawaii, all of the Far East salvage teams were disbanded. Like me, the members of these disbanded salvage teams started looking for new units to join-up with. As a solution to this problem, there was a United States Navy flag ship that needed additional crew members. This flag ship was going back to the States, and it did not have a complete crew. To obtain the needed manpower for the flag ship, a few men out of each salvage crew were taken. About 10 members of my salvage team were able to go back to the United States on this ship. Being on this ship gave me the opportunity to relax after the high stress of salvage. The mission of this flag ship was to transport United States Army units back to the United States. For me and the sailors that had been in my salvage team, the work that we were assigned on the flag ship was relatively stress free.

After arriving in the United States, I took leave, bought a 1948 Mercury convertible, and drove to Perry County, Tennessee. My 1948 Mercury convertible was one of the cars from the previous year's inventory that the dealership had not been able to sell. On November 15, 1949, I returned from leave. Upon my return, I was attached to the Western Pacific Command (WEST PAC) out of Honolulu, Hawaii. This was my first assignment following the Far Eastern Command. The Far Eastern Command had been split up because of the Communist take over of China. When I reported in to WEST PAC, I learned that Fisher had also been assigned to WEST PAC. Being in WEST PAC was great duty compared to being in the Far East (China). However, even in Honolulu, it was dangerous to be outside at night after 11:00 P.M. If you stayed out late at night, you ran the risk of being murdered by the local Japanese, Chinese, or native Hawaiians. Each of these groups harbored great hatred for Americans. There were several explanations for this hostility. First, World War II had just ended, and second, the local inhabitants of the Hawaiian Islands feared that they would soon be dominated by Americans of Western European descent. For these reasons, all sailors in the Hawaiian Islands received what was called Cinderella Liberty (liberty which expired at midnight).

While in WEST PAC, I requested to be made a salvage team crew leader. Because of my prior experience and record from the Far East Command, I received the position. However, the new Salvage Unit Commander indicated that he had some concerns because of my age. As a salvage crew team leader in the Far East, I had become an expert at settling disputes. During a salvage operation, there is no convening authority to turn men over to who were discipline problems. You had to treat these men fairly, but you also had to convince them that it was in their best interest to do their job. In sum, you had to be man enough to force everyone under you to pull their own weight. In my WEST PAC salvage crew, I had a group of men from Iowa and Texas. With these two groups, there was constant bickering. It was a full time job just to keep these two groups from fighting.

There were two positive aspects about the United States Navy's handling of salvage operations. First, the Navy kept track of where we were going, and second, the Navy provided us with accurate information about the inhabitants and diseases that we might encounter on a salvage operation. From my experience, it did not matter where we were going. The Navy would provide detailed information about the terrain and whether there were snakes, crocodiles, cannibals, etc. On many occasions, I would laugh about the information, that the Navy provided. In WEST PAC, most of the ship wreckages that my salvage team recovered were brought to Hunter's Point outside San Francisco, California. However, I did bring one salvaged wreckage back to San Diego, California, just prior to the outbreak of the Korean War.

About six months before the start of the Korean War, I met a Navy Petty Officer by the name of Eagleson. Eagleson was famous for being the sailor who had performed a medical operation on board a submarine while they were sitting at the bottom of Tokyo Harbor during World War II. Petty Officer Eagleson's duty on that submarine eventually damaged his ears so that they leaked fluid. When I met Petty Officer Eagleson, he had ear plugs in to stop this drainage. To my surprise, they had Petty Officer Eagleson sounding the depth of the water along the coast of Korea. He had been tasked with updating the United States Navy maps for the coastline of Korea. When the WEST PAC salvage crews did not have a salvage assignment, they were tasked to assist Petty Officer Eagleson with the sounding and mapping of the Korean coastline, reefs, ports, and tide levels. Petty Officer Eagleson told me while my salvage crew was helping to sound the depth of the waters off the Korean coastline that he had been working on this project for almost a year. After talking with Petty Officer Eagleson, I started putting all the pieces together. It was clear to me that the United States Navy knew that the Korean War was coming almost a year before it started.

I was one of the few men in the United States Navy trained as a United States Navy boat operator (coxswain). Coxswains are specially trained enlisted sailors who command small boats during shore landings and retrieval operations. I had passed my tests and obtained my license as a boat operator prior to becoming a salvage crew team leader in the Far East Command. Being a boat operator came in very handy during salvage operations. Today, boat operators in the United States Navy also command special boat operation units for the Navy SEALs.

CHAPTER 9
SURVIVAL TRAINING

O n February 1, 1950, my salvage crew and I were ordered to go on survival training. I had hoped to avoid the survival training. During the first week of January 1950, all members of the salvage community had received training on how to survive after the sinking of your ship. We were told during this classroom training that some but not all of the salvage teams would be selected to participate in survival training. The classroom presentation on survival training was jam packed with information. I actually was amazed at how much information the Navy had provided in this three hour class.

In preparation for the possibility of surviving the sinking of my ship or for the possibility of being selected to go on survival training, I had prepared a small kit to fit in my pants. I had wrapped the items in the package in plastic and sealed it. In this package, I had cigarette papers, a lighter, and a pocket knife. When they called for my salvage crew and me to go on survival training, we were ordered to report with the clothes on our backs. I grabbed my survival kit and reported topside. All trainees were loaded onto small boats, which departed from the ship for an unknown destination. From the prior reports about survival training, I knew that we would be going to one of two places, Alaska or an island jungle.

When the trainers arrived at the island where we were to conduct the survival training, they dumped me, my salvage crew, and the other sailors included in the training about a mile from shore. In addition, the trainers dumped a specified amount of food, fresh water, and supplies at the same time. Since I was not the senior trainee in terms of rank, I was not in charge of this survival operation. A Lieutenant named Willow was in charge. On my first trip to shore, I brought with me food, water, and supplies. I made three more trips out over a mile from shore to bring in more of the supplies, fresh water, and food that the trainers had left floating in the water where we had been dropped off. After making three and a half round trips over a five hour period, I laid down to rest. While I was resting, Lieutenant Willow came running up and started ranting and raving. I did not know Lieutenant Willow very well, but I knew that he was not a good swimmer. He barely made it to shore with no supplies. Lieutenant Willow said, "We need to gather wood to build a signal fire." The members of my salvage crew were already trying to comply with Lieutenant Willow's orders. After resting a few minutes, I got up. I was not opposed to building a signal fire. In fact, I thought that building a signal fire was a good idea, but I did not feel that it needed to be done immediately. In my mind, the first thing that we needed to do was find drinkable water and to build a shelter from the wind and weather.

Because I had been watching the direction of travel by the small boats that had transported us prior to being dropped off, I had determined that the island selected for our survival training was located somewhere south of the equator. Although I had worked salvage south of the equator, this was not an island that my salvage crew or I were familiar with. I backed from the shore into the water so that I could look at the island. Lieutenant

Willow came up to me and asked "What are you doing?" I told Lieutenant Willow, "I am looking for fresh water." Lieutenant Willow, said, "We will send out a scouting party in the morning." I replied to Lieutenant Willow, "That's fine sir, you do your thing and I will do mine." After locating what appeared to be the greenest part of the foliage on the island, I started through the island underbrush toward that point. The underbrush and canes were thick, but I managed to work my way through the brush to a point higher up on the island. After some searching, I found a spring in the location where the vegetation was the greenest.

About three hours later, I reported back to Lieutenant Willow, "I found fresh water." Lieutenant Willow said, "We are going to build a signal fire, and we will set up camp right here on the beach tonight." I had already seen enough food (bananas, grapes, and coconuts) to live on until we were rescued. I disagreed with Lieutenant Willow, and I told him that I was going to build my shelter up on higher ground closer to the fresh water. Lieutenant Willow said, "Well, you cannot take any of the food and water with you." I replied, "I do not want any of the water or food. You keep it."

If it had not been for my efforts, there would have been very little food, water, and supplies. Almost all of it I had brought ashore. There were ten gallons of fresh water and twenty-five cans of food to share among 40 men. Included within the 40 men were all 17 members of my salvage crew.

I took my survival kit and I turned and said to Lieutenant Willow, "I have no intention of building a shelter on the beach. I am going to build my shelter on high ground." When I made it back to the spring, I went back up the hill from the spring and built a shelter with palm leaves and branches. Next, I went out, cut bananas, gathered honey dew melons and papayas, dug sweet potatoes, and picked grapes. It was not long before Fischer and Peters, two members of my salvage crew, showed up. They said, "We have no confidence in Lieutenant Willow, but we know that you know how to survive."

For the first night of survival training, there were just three living at my camp. We ate bananas, and roasted sweet potatoes. That night I made some lobster traps to catch lobsters. In addition to the abundant fish and shell fish, there was abundant animal life on the island. There were wild goats and wild pigs. To cook the lobsters, I cut off cane and made a cooking pot. Unlike the cane growing near my home in Tennessee, the cane on this island was six to eight inches in diameter. In Tennessee, the largest cane grew along the Buffalo River in Perry County, Tennessee, and it grew to about one inch in diameter. I would cut off a joint of the cane and bury the bottom of the cane in the sand. Then I would build the fire around it. This would allow the fire to heat the water from the sides and kept the fire from burning the bottom out of the cane. By doing this, we could boil water on two separate cookings before being required to replace the cane pot. The lobsters cooked in the makeshift cane pot were not as good as they would have been cooked in a restaurant, but they were mighty fine eating for us during survival training. I would use a sharpened cane to gig flounder. To gig the flounder, I would ease out on the coral reef and locate a pool of water within the coral. As the flounder eased out from the coral, I would slide the sharpened cane spear in the water. Slowly, I would move the cane spear toward the flounder which would be sitting camouflaged on the bottom. Smaller fish of many different colors would be darting around as if in a hurry, but with nowhere to go. Once I had moved the sharpened cane spear to a distance of what appeared to be about 18 inches from the flounder sitting on the bottom, I would make a lightning fast jab. The spear would pierce the flounder and bury about six inches into the sand under the flounder. Once speared, the flounder would attempt to free itself. The water would boil with sand and mud as the flounder fought the spear. It took all my strength to hold the tip of the cane spear buried in the sand. As the flounder continued to fight, it would work itself up the cane toward the surface of the water. After the flounder slid and worked its way up the cane to the surface, I would grab the flounder by the gill and haul it to shore.

I also used the canes to spear the wild goats and wild pigs on the island. The wild goats, after being properly skinned and gutted, turned out to be very good. I would have some of my men rotate the dressed goat on a makeshift spit over the fire. To season the wild goat, I would take salt, which I obtained by letting salt water evaporate on large banana leaves, and sprinkle it on the goat as it slowly roasted over the open fire on the crude spit, which I had made.

My salvage crew and I were on the island for survival training for three weeks. During this time, those who stayed in my camp gained weight. Everyone in my salvage crew was up at my camp within two days after the start of the survival training. In my survival camp, my crew all had sleeping bunks up off the ground. I taught my crew how to build sturdy shelters using the canes and banana leaves.

Five days before the end of the survival training, Lieutenant Willow came up to my camp. He had just about starved eating the survival rations. It was comical to me for Lieutenant Willow to admit he was wrong and to come to my camp. Lieutenant Willow, at the start of the survival training, had lectured me by saying, "Red, you are not a team player and I will not allow you to take any of the food or water rations with you. Soon, you will return from this fool hardiness and I will be here on the beach waiting for you. When we return from this training, I will report your actions to higher authority for appropriate action." I still remember my reply to Lieutenant Willow, "I do not want any part of your food, rations, water, or shelter."

What they taught me during the preparation for survival training was that the goal was to survive at all cost and if I could live 30 minutes longer than the next man, I had a much better chance of being rescued. I went on to tell Lieutenant Willow, "I do not agree with your view of how we are to survive. I intend to utilize all the resources this island has for my survival. Unlike you, I am not going to sit on the beach and wait for rescue."

I had set up simple rules for my camp. Survival was a cooperative effort. Everyone contributed by gathering food, fuel for the fire, drying salt on the banana leaves for seasoning, and obeying the hygiene rules of not taking a bath or going to the bathroom near or around the fresh water spring, which I had located. At my camp, we had no problems, no fighting, and everyone cooperated. All food, like work, was shared.

After the fresh water containers were exhausted, the sailors from the other salvage crews who had stayed on the beach with Lieutenant Willow joined my camp. Everyone in our entire survival unit gained weight. There was no sickness, and most of the men in my camp enjoyed their stay on the island. However, a different survival group on the opposite end of the same island almost starved to death. The United States Navy doctor who came by to check on us daily took the canned food, which Lieutenant Willow had brought to my camp, and delivered it to the other starving unit going through survival training on the opposite end of the island. Because of the shelters that we built, we were not exposed to the weather like the other survival unit. Some of the island storms were fierce. If you got soaked in the rain, you would have to dry out quickly or face the possibility of being chilled and catching a cold. The little island on which we conducted the survival training was about twenty miles in length. I was shocked that anyone could come close to starvation on this island. It was full of fruit and wild animals, which when harvested had allowed my salvage crew and all the sailors in our survival training group to gain weight.

In my camp, we learned from each other. If someone had a better way of doing something, it was adopted by the group.

For example, when I joined the United States Navy, I had never caught a lobster. A member of my salvage crew, Peters, knew how to build a great lobster trap and how to bait it. Peters also knew about abalone and all the other shell fish.

CHAPTER 10
CROSSING THE EQUATOR

T he first time that I crossed the equator was quite an experience. In the United States Navy, the ceremony celebrating crossing the equator was a time honored right of passage. No one knew the exact origin of this ceremony, but it was said to date back to the Vikings who initiated young seaman while on long voyages across the oceans to pillage other lands.

In the United States Navy, it involved an initiation to become what is called a Shellback. The initiation on our ship was a special ceremony. Once a sailor went through the ceremony, that sailor was officially a member of the Order of Shellbacks. Sailors who were not Shellbacks were considered Pollywogs until they had crossed the equator, participated in the special ceremony, and met the challenges set to test their worthiness of earning the Shellback mantle. The ceremony normally involved hours of physical and mental obstacles. After completing the ceremony, a certificate indicating that the sailor was a Shellback was placed in the sailor's service record book. The date and time of that sailor's crossing of the equator was written on the certificate.

All the sailors, including the officers of the ship, who had not crossed the equator and were not Shellbacks were identified. Those sailors who were already Shellbacks had the responsibility of administering the initiation ceremony, and they were armed with shillelaghs to ensure compliance by the Pollywogs. A shillelagh is created by cutting a thirty inch length of fire hose and wrapping one end with a strong fabric to create a handle. Once flattened and soaked in salt water (ocean) the shillelagh becomes firm, yet flexible. For the ceremony on our ship, a big, fat Boatswain Mate had been selected to play the role of King Neptune. This Boatswain Mate's big belly was very hairy. The Shellbacks greased up his belly and painted a face on his belly with lipstick. Next, this Boatswain Mate was placed on a cot, and they smeared raw eggs all over his belly making a slime.

The first right of passage for all who were not Shellbacks was to kiss King Neptune's belly (the fat Boatswain Mate's belly). As I walked up to kiss King Neptune's belly, I felt my stomach get a little queasy. Just as I was ready to place a delicate kiss on the Boatswain Mate's belly, the Boatswain Mate grabbed me and jerked me into his slimy belly. Everyone got a big kick out of seeing those of us crossing the equator for the first time with slime all over our face.

The next part of the initiation was to take a shower to get the slime off your face. When you came out of the shower, you had to go through a belt line. A wet bottom and a leather belt made a good combination. Next, we were marched onto the main deck and thrown over board. Since we were naked when we were thrown overboard, they threw our uniform and shoes overboard with us. This almost seemed too easy. There was just one little catch. You could not come back on board the ship until you were fully dressed. Getting dressed in the water was a real challenge. Some of the sailors almost drowned during this initiation. I helped a few of the weaker swimmers with getting dressed so that they could pass the initiation. Others who failed to get dressed were brought back on board where they went through the initiation process again. Although it did not occur during our Shellback initiation, I had heard of instances where sailors collapsed into tears during the initiation.

CHAPTER 11
SALVAGE OPERATIONS

The USS Askari became the resupply ship and headquarters unit for all the salvage crews in WEST PAC. This ship had changed since the time that I had traveled to Alaska for the expedition to the North Pole. The USS Askari had picked up the nickname, the "slow twenty," and it had become one of the dirtiest ships in the United States Navy.

On my first salvage operation in WEST PAC, my salvage crew and I were tasked with recovering a ship wreckage located near a small island with specific grid coordinates. With these grid coordinates (Longitude and Latitude), the Commander of the Salvage Units expected me to locate the ship wreckage and to bring it back intact or in pieces. What the Salvage Unit Commander failed to tell me was that the ship that I was looking for was located on the top of the island on dry land. In my small boat, I had travelled completely around the island near the grid coordinates four times searching the water for a ship. My salvage crew and I knew the type of ship, and we even had the ship's serial numbers. However, all my searching in the water had been in vain because the ship wreckage was located in the middle of the island. This island was about 150 acres in size with heavy vegetation, which made it very difficult to see anything on the island.

I had checked and rechecked the grid coordinates that were provided. Finally, I decided to call by radio to Headquarters. I told them that we could not find a ship sunk within the vicinity of that particular island. The Duty Officer said, "Stand by, we will get back with you." The next day headquarters called saying, "The location of the ship wreckage has been confirmed, and it is located near the island." I asked, "How far out from the island is the ship supposed to be?" The Duty Officer said, "I do not have that information, but I will get back to you with an answer." In the meantime, I got my salvage crew in my small boat, and we went around the island again looking for this ship wreckage. It was about 50 nautical miles around this island, which was about a two hour run with the small boat. As we went around the island, we stopped and looked at every dark spot or reef in the water. We were just about around the island when headquarters called on the radio to indicate that the ship was not in the water. I said, "Would you repeat that last statement?" Headquarters replied, "The ship is on the island."

Sure enough, when we started looking for the ship wreckage on the island, we found it right away. It was located in the middle of the island. The ship wreckage was well camouflaged by all the tropical vegetation. The island on which this ship was located was covered with palm trees. The only way for this ship to get up in the middle of this island was to get blown up there during a typhoon. To salvage this ship took many steps. First, I had my crew remove the screws (propellers) and the rudder from the ship wreckage. Second, we cut palm tree logs from the island to make a log road from the ship wreckage to the water. It took a while using fire axes to cut enough palm tree logs to make a road to the water. In addition, we did not have the equipment to get up on the beach and move these palm tree logs or the screws and rudder. All this work had to be done by hand. After we got all the palm tree logs in place and greased, we were ready for the third step. During the third step, my salvage crew and I connected cables from the ship wreckage and prepared the cables for future connection to two ships that were in the area (a LST and a LSM(R)). LST was an acronym for Landing Ship, Tank. It was the designation given to a class of United States Navy ships created during World War II to support amphibious operations by carrying significant quantities of vehicles, cargo, and landing troops directly onto an unimproved shore. LSM(R) was an acronym for Landing Ship Medium (Rocket). The LSM(R) was built for the United States Navy to be used during the Battle of Okinawa in World War II. Fourth, I had the Commanders of the LST and the LSM(R) drop their anchors and pay them out as far as they would go. Fifth, my salvage crew and I connected the cables from the ship wreckage on the island to the LST and to the LSM(R). Finally, we were ready to start using the power of the LST and the LSM(R). As I had briefed the commanders of the LST and LSM(R), they were to push away from the island with their engines, while simultaneously taking up the slack in the anchor chain with the anchor winch. Once the ship wreckage got pulled onto the greased palm tree logs everyone had to get out of the way because this ship was headed to the water. Next, my salvage crew and I had to replace the propellers and rudder on the ship wreckage, which now was floating in the ocean. To accomplish this task, my salvage crew and I had to move the propellers and rudder from the top of that island to the shore. Each propeller and the rudder weighed about 1000 pounds. This was a slow and painful process as we slid the propellers and rudder down the greased palm tree logs a little bit at a time to the ocean. We could not hook a cable onto the propellers because they were made out of bronze, and we were afraid that we would break or bend them. However, the real challenge came when we tried to put the screws and rudder back on the ship while sitting in the water just off the coast of this island. If the members of my salvage crew and I had not been outstanding divers, we would never have gotten the screws and rudder back on the ship while at sea. We used a series of cables and come-alongs to maneuver the propellers and rudder into place under the water. A come-along is a small portable winch usually consisting of a cable attached to a hand-operated ratchet. Once we had the propellers and rudder lined up and in place, we fastened them to the ship.

One thing that surprised me about this ship was the fact that there was very little seepage in the ship after being rolled back into the water over the palm tree logs. I thought that there would be some large leaks that would need to be repaired. After we got the propellers and rudder back on the ship, we went to work on the ship's engines. My crew took the engines apart, cleaned them, and replaced damaged parts. The engines ran like new when my crew was finished working on them. The end result was that we sailed this ship back under its own power. What was comical was that after we spent all that time salvaging this ship and repairing it, the United States Government gave the ship to the Japanese. A large number of the ships that my crew and I salvaged were given to the Japanese to become Queen Zeros. We called them Queen Zeros because the serial numbers, which the Japanese put on the ships that we gave them, started off with QO.

Ships that we salvaged, which were in pretty bad shape or which would not run, we took to the port of Sasebo. Sasebo is located on the southern part of mainland Japan. At Sasebo, the Swedish Government sent crews in to cut these ship wreckages up and haul them off. I was not privy to the details or to the arrangement that the United States Government had made with Sweden.

My second salvage job out of WEST PAC took place right in Honolulu Harbor, Hawaii. When I first started my work in salvage, a ship could not be brought straight into Honolulu

Harbor because of the sunken ships and debris in the harbor from World War II. Among the ship wreckages in the harbor was the USS Arizona. My salvage crew would have raised the USS Arizona, but the United States Navy wanted it to be left as a special monument for all to remember the attack on Pearl Harbor. In fact, my crew and I had started preparations to raise the USS Arizona when we were ordered to leave her where she sat. We had already taken her forecastle off in preparation for the salvage operation. We had placed the forecastle on the point of land just down from the location where the USS Arizona was located. The forecastle of a ship, most often spelled as foc'sle to reflect the abbreviated pronunciation used by sailors, is the part of the ship where sailors sleep and congregate while off duty. The foc'sle is located in the forward part of the ship. After we were ordered to stop our salvage operation on the USS Arizona, we did not take the foc'sle back to the Arizona and put it back on.

While we were doing salvage in Honolulu, we would listen to the singing performances in the amphitheater on Saturday nights from our small boat in the harbor. One Saturday night, they had Montana Slim yodeling. Yodeling is a form of singing. It involves singing an extended note, which rapidly and repeatedly changes in pitch from the chest voice making a high-low-high-low sound. The English word yodel originally came from a German word jodeln meaning "to utter the syllable jo" (pronounced "yo" in English). I will never forget how incredible Montana Slim's yodeling sounded as it echoed over the water. Montana Slim could really yodel!

During all of my salvage operations both in the Far East and in WEST PAC, I always worked for an officer who assigned the salvage missions. However, not one of these officers ever came out to a salvage location. The only person who ever came out to the salvage locations was the corpsman. When my salvage crew and I saw a corpsman coming, we knew to get ready to take all of our shots again. It seemed like every time that a mass epidemic of some disease killed off a few thousand people in India or China that the corpsman would show up to vaccinate my salvage crew and me for those diseases.

Probably the salvage operation that I enjoyed the most involved a Japanese ship wreckage, which the Japanese and Australians had both failed to remove. This Japanese ship wreckage was blocking Tokyo Harbor. Part of the ship was sticking up out of the water because the water was not deep enough to cover the ship all the way. To salvage this ship, my salvage crew and I first checked the compartments of this Japanese wreckage to see if any of them were water tight (without holes). Next, my salvage crew installed two pipes with valves going to each of the water tight compartments, which we had located. Through one pipe we pumped air, and the other pipe provided an avenue of escape for the water as the air pressure inside the compartment increased. After forcing the water out and putting air pressure in these water tight compartments, I had my salvage crew cut the valves off on both pipes for each water tight compartment. Next, we attached deflated causeways with very little air pressure to the sides of the ship wreckage with cables. After connecting the causeways, I had my salvage crew gradually increase the air pressure in the causeways. As the air pressure in the causeways increased, more lift was exerted by the causeways to bring the ship up. Since the ship was lodged in the mud and sediment, we also set small explosives around the base of the ship to jolt or knock the ship loose from the bottom. Each of these small explosive charges consisted of a two inch piece of dynamite. In addition, I had my salvage crew attach two warping tugs to put lateral pressure on the ship wreckage. When everything was ready, I set off the charges. Everyone watching the salvage operation was surprised at how high this ship shot out of the water. The water movement, caused by this ship shooting to the surface, created a surface wave twelve feet high inside the harbor. I was on the warping tug when I set off the charges, and the Japanese ship wreckage popped to the surface. The wave that this Japanese ship wreckage caused flipped my tool box and tools off the warping tug and into the harbor. We were able to recover some of my tools and the tool box, but once the tools got into the mud they were very difficult to find.

Once this Japanese ship wreckage was on the surface, we carefully examined it. The hole in this Japanese ship wreckage was very small, and it should never have sunk. If there had been an engineer damage control unit on this Japanese ship, they should have been able to seal off the damaged compartment until repairs could be made. Based upon my analysis, this Japanese ship did not sink until the Japanese Commander ran it aground. In sum, it should not have sunk from being torpedoed. The water where this Japanese ship sunk was only 60 or 70 feet deep.

Another project, which we undertook in Tokyo Harbor, was the removal of the submarine nets. Across Tokyo Harbor they had a steel webbed net, which they could open and close to protect the ships in the harbor. The web netting was to prevent a submarine from sitting outside the harbor and sinking ships inside the harbor. The torpedoes would explode when they struck the steel netting. Evidently, several torpedoes had struck this netting because it was torn to pieces. My salvage crew and I had to cut the remaining portions of this netting and pull it out of the harbor. We turned all of this salvaged netting over to the Japanese.

For every piece of property, which we salvaged, paperwork and forms had to be completed. This paperwork explained what item was salvaged, where it was salvaged, and who the salvaged property belonged to. During my next salvage operation in Tokyo Harbor, we salvaged several pieces of property claimed by the Japanese. For example, while on this salvage operation, we found three one man submarines. The Japanese, when they learned that we had located these submarines, demanded their return. The United States Navy became concerned that the Japanese military officials would seek retribution against the Japanese military personnel who allegedly operated these submarines. To prevent this retribution, we were ordered to remove all the serial numbers from the one-man submarines. If the Japanese military could trace who was in charge of these submarines, they would have ordered their execution for failing to destroy them prior to their abandonment.

Another key salvage operation, which my crew performed, occurred near a place called Enewetak. Enewetak was the name given to an atoll located at the northwestern end of the Ralik chain of the Republic of the Marshall Islands in the Pacific Ocean. To me Enewetak atoll appeared to be the top of an extinct volcano. It was comprised of around 40 small islands that ringed a circular lagoon 23 miles in diameter. During World War II, Enewetak was captured from the Japanese in 1944 by the United States. It offered excellent anchorage, and it was made into a United States naval base. The inhabitants of Enewetak were evacuated to other atolls after it was designated with Bikini atoll as a testing ground for United States atomic weapons.

The salvage operation at Enewetak involved a ship that was literally split in half and sitting on the bottom of the lagoon. The water in the lagoon was shallow enough that the two parts of the ship were not totally under water. After sealing off several air tight compartments in each of the two halves, we forced the water out of each of the air tight compartments using the two pipes with valves. Next, my salvage crew and I managed to dislodge and re-float each half. Because the Lieutenant who had assigned me this salvage operation wanted to discredit me, he had ordered me to bring this ship wreckage into Honolulu Harbor in Hawaii. The Lieutenant made one serious mistake. He put the orders that he gave me in writing and signed them. Since my salvage crew and I had no radio communication to request assistance, we were forced to sail the two halves of this ship wreckage into Honolulu Harbor as set forth in my orders. On this odyssey, my salvage crew and I rode the stern half while we towed the bow half bobbing up and down behind us. It probably looked like an ugly parade when we came sailing into Honolulu Harbor.

Working to salvage ship wreckages is a real challenge. In fact, it is a challenge to do anything underwater. Everyone should try working underwater just for the experience. Underwater it is often necessary to have someone hold you to keep you from moving while you are trying to work. For example, every time you would push on something underwater instead of it giving you would give. Tasks, which would be simple on the surface such as cutting a hole in a half inch piece of steel, would be almost impossible or take a tremendous period of time. In the late 1940's and early 1950's the equipment we used, although state of the art, was poor by today's standards. In addition, most of our equipment operated off of pure muscle power and not motors. To cut a two inch hole in a plate of one half inch steel underwater required substantial preparation. The first man down would start the process of welding feet pieces to hold his body in place. After completing this process, the next task would be to clamp the manual cutter to the steel plate to be cut. Finally, the process of turning the cutting mechanism by hand would be ready to begin. All of these procedures take a tremendous amount of time. The time factor was compounded by the fact that each diver only could remain underwater 30 minutes at a time. Most of the work underwater required at least two divers working together. For example, putting a clevis on something and tightening it up with a marlin spike was almost impossible by yourself. What would happen is that you would start turning rather than the clevis. Doing this type of work would wear you out because you were fighting against yourself.

To help with the salvage of ship wreckages, an inventor came up with the idea of lead plugs to seal small holes in the ship's compartments. To install these lead plugs, a sledge hammer was used to drive them into the holes. Once the lead was in the hole it acted like a gasket. Above water, pounding lead plugs into holes was easy. Furthermore, the lead worked like a charm to seal the hole. However, underwater it was a totally different story. Striking a lead plug with a sledge hammer underwater was an impossibility. Even trying to swing a hammer underwater was dangerous because you might strike yourself or another diver. Ultimately, getting the lead plug into the hole underwater was a major accomplishment. The best tool that we had in salvage at that time was the router cutter which you turned around and around by hand. After cutting the hole in the water tight compartment, we would install two pipes. One of the pipes would run to just a few inches from the bottom of the water tight compartment. The second pipe would be installed just a few inches below the top of the water tight compartment. Both pipes would have valves outside the water tight compartment. The pipe at the top of the water tight compartment would be used to provide the air intake. The pipe near the bottom of the water tight compartment would be used to provide the out take. Around the two pipes going into the holes entering into the water tight compartment, we placed a special metal and rubber gasket. The base of this gasket was a solid piece. The top of the gasket consisted of two parts, which fit around the pipes and bolted into place. As air was pumped through the intake pipe, the pressure in the compartment increased and the water in the compartment would be forced out by the air. When the pipe near the bottom of the compartment started blowing air, the valves on each of the pipes were turned off.

Many times, while my salvage crew and I were working on a salvage operation, a bell would be lowered to the 60 foot level. Fresh air would be pumped from the surface into the diving bell. Instead of returning to the surface after spending about

30 minutes working, we would go to the diving bell. Working out of a diving bell ultimately causes problems with your sinus cavities and joints.

Each salvage project that I was assigned was unique. I never got bored. New obstacles arose with each project. Usually, the salvage projects we received involved those, which were too difficult for others to accomplish. When we were on a salvage project, we did not receive hot chow. Often, we were one to two hundred miles from our resupply command ship. In effect, we operated on our own, and the only person from our command ship who came out to visit us was the corpsman.

With all the salvage operations, which my salvage crew and I conducted, we were lucky that we never had anyone killed or seriously injured. However, a member of my salvage crew was killed during a routine yard inspection, which we were performing. Because of my yard rating, I had been requested to make a yard inspection of a United States Navy cargo ship (LSD) located near the equator. The term LSD is the acronym for Landing Ship, Dock. This ship can best be described as an amphibious warfare ship with a well dock to transport and launch landing craft and amphibious vehicles. This LSD also had bow doors to enable it to deliver vehicles directly to a beach like a LST. Because of its design a LSD could transfer cargo to landing craft in rougher seas than a ship that has to use cranes or a stern ramp.

My inspection was to determine whether or not there was a reason for this LSD to go into the yard for repair. When I went on board this LSD with my salvage crew, we found several problems with the equipment being used. Different tags were used to indicate how serious the problem was. If the piece of equipment just needed to be tightened up, a white tag would be used. When I found a problem that was dangerous and likely to cause death or injury, I placed a red tag on it. I had put a red tag on the spindle winch because I felt this piece of equipment was extremely dangerous since the switch on the motor to the winch, which was part of a crane, would not cut off. This spindle winch motor was primarily used to tighten the cable for lifting and moving cargo. The only way the motor to the spindle winch could be cut off was to pull the breaker or to shut off the power to the spindle winch motor from the ship's engine room.

In addition to this particular piece of equipment, I had red tagged several other pieces of equipment. After completing the yard inspection on the LSD, I was talking to the Engineering Officer on the LSD about the need for them to have repairs made at the closest naval yard. For this inspection, I was not dressed in a uniform showing my grade. Since I worked in salvage, I was in the habit of wearing a working uniform. I guess that I probably did not look the part of an inspector. I had on dungarees, a pair of tennis shoes, and no shirt. Maybe the crew of the LSD thought that I did not look like an inspector. Whether it was the way I was dressed or for some other reason, my decision to red tag the spindle winch was not respected. Right after I got finished talking to the Engineering Officer, I came back up on the main deck and witnessed a member of the LSD crew operating the piece of equipment, which I had just red tagged. I asked the operator, "Who took the red tag off this piece of equipment?" The operator said, "I did." I told the operator, "This machine is dangerous. You cannot stop it." The operator ignored my warning and continued to use this machine to reel in cable. Well, just as I had predicted the machine failed to shut off. It kept tightening the cable it was reeling in. Suddenly, the cable snapped! When the cable snapped, it sailed through the air striking a sailor named Tubby McMillian from my salvage team. This cable cut Tubby McMillian in half like a knife going through hot butter. When McMillian was struck, he had a set of headphones on, and he was laughing. Even after the cable cut McMillian in two he was still laughing. After this accident, everyone wanted to blame someone else for McMillian's death.

On my inspection report, which I had already delivered to the Engineering Officer, I had indicated that the spindle winch motor was dangerous and that I had red tagged it. The operator who had removed my red tag and continued to operate the spindle winch had done so on orders from his Lieutenant. Both the Lieutenant and the enlisted operator were charged with manslaughter for causing the death of Tubby McMillian. I was called to testify at the court-martial of the Lieutenant. The attorney representing the Lieutenant wanted to know where I got my expertise. I told them, "I did not know that I was an expert. I was just doing my job, but I can tell if a switch will shut off or on. This switch simply did not work." The Lieutenant was convicted of manslaughter, sentenced to 5 years of hard labor, and dishonorably discharged.

I was very upset because of the death of Tubby McMillian. From experience, I learned that there will always be people in this world like the Lieutenant. I never really cared whether a man was an officer or not. If he could offer some good advice, I was always willing to listen.

Because of my desire to learn, I found myself seeking out those local natives who could teach me about their uncanny ability to travel from island to island. I would spend hours talking to them about their travels, and how they accomplished such feats. For example, I was fascinated by the Kanaka islanders who were sailing around in makeshift boats from island to island picking coconuts in the South Pacific. Kanaka is a word used to refer to the Polynesian peoples who live in the Melanesian countries such as New Caledonia. I had the best equipment that the United States Navy could buy, and I still had trouble finding some of the islands. But one of the island natives whom I nicknamed "Grandpa" taught me how I could tell when I was getting near an island. Grandpa showed me how the water changed color as you approached the island. The water changes from a deep, dark blue color to a lighter blue, to a lighter blue green as you approach an island. As the water turned to a lighter blue green you could start to see coral. The coral was dangerous in places because of the possibility of damaging the bottom of your ship.

I had an old Chinese man named Chiangshaw tell me something that I have never forgotten. The first time that I met Chiangshaw was when my crew and I had were assigned to salvage a ship wreckage in the Far East off the coast of China. Chiangshaw came up to my crew, and he asked for something. I gave the item that Chiangshaw asked for to him. When I gave Chiangshaw what he asked for, he made the statement, "Cumshaw cumshaw is OK, but cumshaw cumshaw all the time is not good." Cumshaw as used by Chiangshaw meant "you give to me." This term originated from the old Chinese term "kam sia" meaning "grateful thanks." After thinking about what Chiangshaw said for a long time, I now understand what he was trying to tell me. Chiangshaw meant that if a person just keeps asking for someone to give him something, there is something wrong with this person's character.

My salvage crew was selected for a dangerous salvage operation in New Guinea. New Guinea is located in the southwest Pacific Ocean. It lies geographically to the east of the Malay Archipelago, and it is the world's second largest island, after Greenland. The briefers and my Salvage Unit Commander told me that the two previous salvage crews that had been assigned to salvage this ship had disappeared in New Guinea without a trace. The briefers made a special effort to explain about the culture of the local tribes near the salvage site. According to this brief, the local tribes near the salvage site were known to be head-hunters. Of the two previous salvage crews, all that was ever found was the small boats, which were being used by these crews. These small boats were found beached near the base camp established by these salvage crews. Based on the disappearance of both of these salvage crews, the briefers recommended that my salvage crew and I limit contact with the local natives. What I took away from this information was that the two previous salvage crews had been eaten by the local head-hunters and cannibals.

In the past, the Navy briefers had been very accurate and truthful about what to expect from the local inhabitants, wildlife, and plant life surrounding each salvage area. On past missions, I had been informed about giant sea turtles, sharks, and barracudas that might be found around the ship wreckage. During my past briefs, the Navy briefers pulled no punches. In those briefs, I learned about poisonous snakes, the diseases common to the region, the sexual diseases carried by the natives, and the religious practices. As with past missions, I passed this information about the salvage site at New Guinea to my salvage crew. No matter how silly or unusual the information, I explained to my crew that our mission was to complete the salvage of the ship wreckage in New Guinea.

Upon arriving at the salvage sight in New Guinea with my salvage team, I beached our small boat near a sandbar extension running out from the beach. The beach near the salvage area stretched approximately 500 yards before becoming a tangled jungle of trees, vines, caves, and underbrush. The sand on the beach was the purest white color that I had ever seen. In fact, the beach was incredibly beautiful. To protect my base camp on the salvage effort, I set up a 50 caliber machine gun for security. I made a mark in the sand about 300 yards from the shore. I told the guards that I put on the 50 caliber machine gun not to allow any of the inhabitants or natives to cross the mark I made in the sand. If the inhabitants or natives tried to cross this mark, the guards were to fire the 50 caliber machine gun in the sand in front of them and plow a furrow in the sand to convince them to go back. Two hours later, some of the natives attempted to cross the mark that I had made in the sand. The guard on the 50 caliber fired a series of rounds into the sand in front of the approaching natives. The rounds hitting the beach threw sand all over the approaching natives. The natives instantly turned and ran back into the woods. After this incident, the natives tried to come out to talk to me and my crew. To make sure there was no misunderstanding, I walked out to talk to the chief of the local tribe. I told the chief, "My crew and I are not here to hurt you or your people." I explained to the chief, "My job is to clean up the beach and to salvage the United States Navy ships. Your people are not to come onto the beach where we are working or near any of my crew." The local natives in this part of New Guinea had certain traditions. The young women with red flowers in their hair were looking for husbands, and the young women with white flowers in their hair were too young to be married. However, what amazed me were the women natives who had children. These women were able to nurse their children while their children were standing on the ground. Some of these native women had breasts which seemed to be almost a foot in length. All the natives in New Guinea were naked, and I do not think they had ever worn any clothing.

From my perspective, the friendliness of the natives was a ploy. In my mind, that was how the natives got close enough to over-power and kill the first two salvage crews. Some of the natives could speak very good English. When I asked about the whereabouts of the other two crews, the natives responded, "I do not know." This answer made me very skeptical. I knew deep down in my bones that the natives were lying. I thought to myself. I am not going to let any of the natives get close enough to grab me or any of my crew. In fact, I made it crystal clear to my salvage crew that no one was allowed to leave the beach base camp. To obtain fruit and water to augment the sea rations, I went to one of the nearby uninhabited islands. My salvage crew and I were very concerned about not eating or drinking anything provided by the local natives because of the fear of being drugged or poisoned. My crew was not a bunch of saints, but the natives knew that my salvage crew and I meant what we said. In fact, the local chief went back and brought a French diplomat with him. The French diplomat named Pierre said, "Your crew has been very impolite by refusing the hospitality of the chief and by firing the 50 caliber machine gun at the chief's people when they came out to greet you." I replied to Pierre, "Stay on the other side of the mark and we will remain friendly. I will talk to you from a safe distance, and we do not want to go to dinner."

After the salvage operation in New Guinea, my crew and I were sent on a special mission to Port Arthur, Russia. The city of Port Arthur is located on the southern extremity of the Liaodong Peninsula commanding the entrance to the Bohai Gulf. The Russians had lost this port city to the Japanese. However, when the Japanese surrendered at the end of World War II, the Russians quickly moved back into Port Arthur to loot the industrial base Japan had built in Manchuria. Russian troops occupied the Liaodong area until 1950 when Russia returned Port Arthur to China. Port Arthur is now called Lushun City. My salvage crew was ordered to help bring back the first ship from the Soviet Union, which the United States had provided to the Soviets during World War II. Several ships were brought back after this one, but my crew went into Port Arthur to get the first ship.

After seeing what the Russians had done to this ship that my salvage crew and I were assigned to recover, I changed my opinion of the Russians. There was filth all over this ship. The Russians had gone to the bathroom in the corners of the rooms on the ship instead of using the commodes. On all the engines and controls, the Russians had put Russian name plates. No one in my crew had any tools, although each of us had a tool box. Each tool box was full of small arms and ammunition. When I was briefed on this mission, I had been told that the prior salvage team sent to bring back this ship had gone into Russia but never returned. Our intent was to kill a large number of the Russians if they tried to stop us from bringing the ship back. The rumor was that the prior crews, which had disappeared in the Soviet Union, were being used by the Soviets for experimentation.

The group that my salvage crew and I joined up with for this mission consisted of about 40 men. It was kind of comical when our group went aboard the ship to be recovered in Port Arthur. A Soviet Naval officer approached our group. The Navy had issued us all new uniforms. We had no names in our uniforms, and we had no forms of identification. Everyone was dressed exactly the same. The Soviet Naval officer, speaking English, requested for the officer-in-charge (OIC) to step forward. I looked at my crew, and no OIC stepped forward. No one laughed. No one coughed, and no one moved. Everyone had a tool box. My tool box had two grease guns, about 1000 rounds of ammunition, and several knives. I was in charge of the engineers, but I was not in charge of this operation. I did not ask, and I did not want to know who was the OIC. No one admitted that they were in charge or would step forward. The Russian Officer stated, "Well alright." We were escorted to a barracks where we spent the night. My crew and I did not sleep at all that night. If any of the Russians had entered the barracks that night, they would have been killed. My crew consisted of 17 men, and we were prepared to fight our way out of the Soviet Union if it had been required. I did not think that the rest of my crew had done the same thing I had done. I thought surely my crew had some tools in their tool boxes. However, when we got on the ship the next morning and started trying to get the ship's engines going, I learned that I was wrong. While working on one of the engines, I turned to Fisher and said, "I need a screw driver." Fisher looked at me and said, "Did you bring a tool box?" I answer, "Yes, but the screw driver is gone." Fisher said, "I never did have a screw driver." Fisher's tool box, like mine, was full of small arms and ammunition. In particular, Fisher had a 10 gauge sawed off shotgun. I smiled at Fisher as he said, "Where are your tools?" I responded, "I have the tools of my trade in that tool box." Fisher just laughed and said, "Yes, and that tool box contains the tools of my trade." I started looking around and out of the 17 men in my crew, there was not a single tool. Each member of my crew had a tool box full of weapons and ammunition.

I had to improvise and use a pocketknife in lieu of a screw driver. Another obstacle facing my crew and me was that the equipment in the engine rooms was pre-World War II vintage. This along with all the directions written in Russian made working in the engine room even more difficult. However, despite these problems, my crew and I had the engines up and running in no time.

The Russians never gave us any trouble. In my own mind, I think the Russians knew by looking at our group that this was not a crew that they should try to stop. My salvage crew would have killed every Russian up there to bring back this ship. Joe Monday, a member of my salvage crew, was always spoiling for a fight, and he was definitely ready to fight the Russians. My crew lived for trouble. There were two Singleton brothers (Mark and Henry) in my salvage crew, and they loved to fight. I had warned my crew that I would not stay in Russia and that I would not be captured. My crew knew from experience that if anyone crowded me or pressured me, it would be hazardous to their health. Everyone in my crew also knew that if the Russians tried to stop us that I would come out fighting. The first night I wanted to go over to the ship, but the Russians directed us to the barracks. I did not know whether I should start something or not, but I just played it cool and went over to the barracks to spend the night. However, I had every intention of leaving the next morning, when I got up. The Russian Officer had said, "I will take you to the ship for an inspection in the morning, and then you may leave." My salvage crew and I had been selected for this mission because of our reputation for being able to complete any task assigned. Also, we had the reputation of being one of the toughest crews in the United States Navy. In fact, my crew was known for fighting anyone who wanted a fight, and we always won the fight.

When I thought back over these missions in my mind, I felt deep within my soul that if I had let the New Guinea natives into our camp, they would have eaten us for dinner, and likewise, the Russians would have had us mining salt or being experimental guinea pigs. I learned that the key to success was to show the other side that you were the boss. I knew in my heart that the men on the other side could read the determination in my face and the faces of my crew. When I looked a man in the eyes, I could always tell if he was going to be trouble, and I am sure the Chief of the New Guinea tribes as well as the Russian Officer could too.

The quartermaster bringing the ship for recovery out of the Soviet Naval Base in Port Arthur was a member of my salvage crew. He was a fellow by the name of George Willingham from Dallas, Texas. George Willingham had an amazing ability to judge distance, and he could easily guide a large ship through the eye of a needle. If I had to depend on someone to drive a ship through a small opening, George Willingham was the man I would put behind the wheel.

For a short time, my salvage crew and I worked out of the Navy ship yards in Yokohama, Japan. All the crews working in the Navy Yard in Yokohama were billeted in the barracks. Who went first in the chow line was determined by the barracks you were assigned. A Scottish Highlander unit was billeted in one of the farthest barracks from the chow hall. Every morning, when the Scots would come down to the chow hall for breakfast, my crew and I would be returning from breakfast. Members of my crew would start hollering at the Scots as they marched to breakfast in their kilts. One morning, John Singleton yelled at the Scottish unit, "What do you have under your skirt?" The Scots were playing their bagpipes and drums and marching along, but the statement by John Singleton started a brawl. After that morning, it seemed like we fought the Scots every morning. Any unit caught fighting was not allowed to go to chow for breakfast. However, my crew and I had already eaten. The poor Scots must have been starving because they never got to eat breakfast since they were always fighting with my crew. It was almost like a ritual. My salvage crew would shout insults at the Scots until the Scots would break rank and start a brawl with my crew.

I always enjoyed talking to the Scottish and Australian service members. If you were red headed the Australians would call you "Blue." All the maritime countries would send out crews to watch us and observe the techniques of my salvage crew during salvage operations. It was not unusual to have two or three crews from the western European countries watching us conduct a salvage operation. Often my crew would conduct a salvage operation in a series of steps. As we conducted each step of the salvage operation, we would allow the divers from the other countries to go down to see what we had done. Whenever possible, I would take the salvage jobs, which were difficult and farther away from bases to avoid the side show for the foreign salvage crews.

During salvage operations, if I needed a piece of equipment not available in the area, I would go to my friend, J. B. Smith, who was aboard the USS Mount McKinley. Often, I would blackmail J. B. Smith into getting the equipment I needed. If I came aboard the Mount McKinley in my dungaree uniform, it would get J. B. Smith in trouble because of the way I was dressed. To keep me from coming aboard, J. B. Smith would do almost anything. The USS Mount McKinley was the Flag ship, and the Captain of the USS Mount McKinley wanted all sailors dressed in the Class A uniform. There was no way I could put on a Class A uniform since on a salvage operation all we had were dungarees, shorts, and diving gear. Many times the Salvage Unit Commander or resupply command ship would be several hundred miles from the location of the salvage site. In addition, in the hot humid weather around the equator our clothes would wear out faster and start to rot because of the heat and moisture.

While working salvage missions, it was not uncommon for my crew and me to go for months without being paid. On salvage operations my crew and I needed no money since there was no place to spend it even if you had it. The monkeys did not sell coconuts and the parrots did not sell bananas. There were no cities or stores. Most of the islands where we worked had very few inhabitants or were uninhabited. On salvage operations, my crew and I would watch the natives going around to harvest coconuts. Getting into the coconut is not easy. My crew and I would take a fire axe and try to chop our way into them. The natives had a unique way of getting into the coconuts. They would bury a stick deep in the sand and tamp it tightly. This stick would be beveled on the top. The native who was hulling the coconuts would sit astride of the stick. He would take a coconut in both hands and strike the end of the coconut that had been fastened onto the tree against the beveled end of the stick buried in the sand. As the native struck the coconut against the stick, he would twist the coconut with his hands and the hull would pop off. A skilled native could hull coconuts as fast as he could pick them up. After watching the natives, I got where I could hull coconuts just like the natives. Another interesting technique used by the natives was how they cut bananas. When a banana ripens on the tree, it turns red. A banana, which has ripened on the tree, is like a laxative. To obtain a banana that you could eat, the banana had to be cut from the tree while it was green and allowed to ripen.

CHAPTER 12
MESS DUTY

On my last salvage operation, I was ordered to bring a ship wreckage that my crew had salvaged in the western Pacific Ocean to San Diego, California. At the time, I did not know that this was going to be my final salvage operation. After docking the ship wreckage in the Naval Ship Yards in San Diego, my salvage crew and I were sent to the San Diego Naval Base to await transportation back to WEST PAC. During my time in the Navy, I had been in and out of the Naval Base at San Diego about fifteen times, and over this period, I had become very curious about what was going on in building 5. All military installations, including San Diego Naval Base, had regulations and orders, which required that all the lights in all buildings would be turned off at 11:00 P.M., except for buildings where it was necessary for them to be on. I had noticed during my past visits to the San Diego Naval Base, that at 2:00 A.M. and 3:00 A.M. in the morning building 5 would be lit up like a Christmas tree. I always wondered why they had the lights on. Well, when I received my assignment to mess duty, I found out why those lights were on. There were about a hundred of us that reported onto San Diego Naval Base that day. As a salvage team crew leader, my position carried a little prestige. However, at the formation held that evening, a Chief Petty Officer came out, walked down the front of the formation, and said, "From here back report to building 5." What I soon learned was that all sailors without an entry in their service record book covering mess cooking were fair game to be assigned to mess duty even if they were crew leaders. There were two duties that all sailors had to do: (1) department cleaning and (2) mess cooking. Department cleaning consisted of cleaning the sleeping compartments and the barracks common areas to include the heads (bathrooms).

At the time that I was assigned mess duty, there were about 30,000 sailors and other military personnel on board the Naval Base at San Diego. We were going to be the cooks in the mess facility for all of these people. We had the responsibility to cook three meals a day for all of these service members. My first job as a cook was to prepare cauliflower for 30,000 service members. The first cauliflower that I ever saw I cooked. So you know that this cauliflower had to be good. What was really comical was that they sent me back into the fruit and vegetable locker to get the cauliflower. I thought that they would have the name written on the box so that I could find it. After looking all over the locker, I could not find a box saying cauliflower. I saw a large number of boxes, which had these funny looking white heads on them. From the fruit and vegetable locker, there was a small train to carry the vegetables to the main kitchen for preparation. The serving size for cauliflower was one quarter of a pound per person, approximately 7500 pounds of cauliflower. The fruit and vegetable locker alone was a building about 250 feet long by 200 feet wide.

Being unable to locate the cauliflower, I returned to the chief cook, and I said, "Can you please help me find the cauliflower?" The chief cook walked down to the fruit and vegetable locker with me and pointed out the cauliflower and said, "All that is cauliflower, sailor. Get enough for one quarter of a pound for everyone on the base." I got the train as close as I could to the cauliflower and loaded up enough boxes to equal a little over 7500 pounds.

When I brought the cauliflower up to the kitchen, the Chief cook said, "Use those two big caldrons to your left." I looked to my left and there were two of the biggest stainless steel pots that I had ever seen in my life. These pots were about twelve feet in diameter with ladders welded on the side. I climbed up the ladder on the side of each pot, and I filled each of these pots about two thirds of the way full of cauliflower. Since I had never cooked cauliflower, I had no idea what I was doing. By this time, it was getting close to dinner time. I did not wash this cauliflower off or cut it up before putting it in these pots because I was running out of time. After filling up these pots, I asked the Chief cook, "What do I do next?" He replied, "Put the steam to it." I did exactly what he said. Finally, we got through with this first meal. The next job that I received was to cook potatoes. For potatoes, the United States Navy had a piece of equipment, which would hold about 500 pounds of potatoes at one time. I poured the potatoes through the top of the machine. As the potatoes were poured in, water was constantly running through the machine. By the time the potatoes came out the bottom, they were peeled. If the potatoes were held in the machine for any time at all, the water would grind them down until they would not be as big as the end of your thumb. I was supposed to cut the bad spots out of them as they came out, but I was too busy just trying to get enough potatoes peeled and cooked to feed 30,000 service members.

The next morning, I was placed on the serving line cooking eggs to order. I was assigned to a grill, which was about thirty feet long and four feet wide. It was all I could do to reach the far side of the grill with a spatula. The Chief cook told me to break eggs on the grill. So I started breaking eggs on the grill. The serving per person was two eggs. So that meant that I had to break 60,000 eggs for the breakfast meal. The old Master at Arms overseeing the serving line was from White County, Tennessee. He came up to me and said, "By God Red, we do not have a week to feed them. We are going to have breakfast over by 7:00 A.M." I said, "What do you mean?" He said, "Break those eggs like this." The Master at Arms reached in there and got three eggs in each hand and broke them on the grill all in one motion without breaking any of the yolks. I told him, "I cannot do that." He said, "You damn sure will. Now get after it." I reached in there and brought out three eggs in each hand. The first few times I got scrambled eggs and hulls on the grill, but it was not long before I could break six eggs at a time on the grill. In addition to the eggs, we cooked bacon and sausage. It would take hours to place the bacon in the pans the night before so that it could be run into the oven to be cooked the next morning. I learned that placing the bacon in the pans at night was the reason the lights were on all night in building 5. Depending upon, which detail you were assigned, the time required for the preparation and cooking of the meal varied. I had to stay on mess cook detail for thirty days. But the training that I received during this thirty day period was invaluable. Being on mess duty simply developed a good foundation, which I later could build on. Today, I feel confident that I can cook with the best.

One of the problems that we faced on mess duty was that the individuals making out the menus had no common sense. For example, they would make a menu calling for T-bone steak. The problem is that there are only four T-bone steaks in a cow. To serve 30,000 service members T-bone steak, we would need 15,000 sides of beef. What the menu should have said was steak instead of T-bone steak. However, while cutting meat, I learned how to make rib steak, porter house steak, and other types of steaks look like a T-bone. By using tooth picks and splitting a few bones, I could cut twenty-four good T-bone steaks out of one cow. For the individual who does not know how the T-bone muscle should look, I can cut approximately sixty T-bone steaks out of one cow. I could cut steaks and by using a few toothpicks make them look like T-bones.

Whenever the menu called for meat, you had to have half a pound per service member. Sometimes they would come out with a crazy menu requiring center cut pork chops. You can get two center cut pork chops per hog. For 30,000 service members to each get a center cut pork chop you would need 15,000 hogs. As you can imagine, I became very creative when it came to cutting meat!

Our menu varied during the 30 days that I was on mess duty. In addition to the traditional pancakes, eggs to order, bacon, and sausage breakfast, we served corned beef hash; beans and corn bread; cream beef and hash brown potatoes. Our group became very good at preparing a wide variety of food. All types of seasonings were available to flavor the food that we cooked. The hardest meal to prepare was breakfast. The lunch and supper meals were pretty easy because it was simply a matter of baking or roasting things in ovens.

CHAPTER 13

REPAIR OF LST 845

S ome of the subordinate officers that I had worked for in the Navy Salvage Command had tried to make me look bad by giving me salvage jobs, which were considered impossible. In some cases, I had been tasked with salvage operations that multiple salvage crews had failed to complete. However, my salvage record was unblemished. I completed all the salvage operations that I had been assigned. Everyone in WEST PAC knew that my salvage crew was the best. After the start of the Korean conflict, my salvage crew and I did not salvage any more ship wreckages.

My three year term of voluntary service in the United States Navy was set to expire, and I had over 60 days of leave on the books. This leave, when combined with travel time and discharge processing time, meant that I would be allowed to go on terminal leave over three months before my actual discharge date. With only three months to go before the end of my enlistment, I had notified the Commander of the Navy Salvage Unit that I would be leaving salvage and that I would be processed out of the United States Navy at Treasure Island, California. At the time, I was mustering out of the Navy, it took about two weeks to complete the discharge paperwork and physical. Practically my entire salvage crew was with me going through processing for discharge to get out of the Navy.

While I was at Treasure Island awaiting the finalization of the paperwork for my discharge, I received a message that Lieutenant Commander Gusparidge had called. I knew Lieutenant Commander Gusparidge during my Far East salvage operations. At the time that I first met Lieutenant Commander Gusparidge, he was a Lieutenant.

When I returned Lieutenant Commander Gusparidge's call, he asked, "Have you been discharged yet?" and I told him, "No." He told me, "You know if you get out of the Navy, they are going to draft you as soon as you get home." Lieutenant Commander Gusparidge asked me, "Have you been keeping up with the news lately?" I said, "Not really!" Lieutenant Commander Gusparidge explained, "The North Koreans have crossed over the 38th parallel. Looks like there will be a police action in Korea. They are going to give me a ship. I would like to have you and your salvage team as part of my ship's crew if possible." I told Lieutenant Commander Gusparidge, "I really need to go home." Lieutenant Commander Gusparidge responded, "Well take some leave and go home, but you need to let me know before you go on leave. How long will it be before your discharge is finalized?" I said, "Two or three days." Lieutenant Commander Gusparidge said, "Well, let me know something before you are discharged."

To check up on how things were going concerning the draft in Tennessee, I called the Perry County Sheriff's office. Atlas Webb was the Sheriff of Perry County. Atlas Webb sent Jack Bates over on Brush Creek to get my mother to call me back. When my mother called me, she told me that Bobby Hinson and Atha Trull both got out of the Navy two weeks ago, and both were drafted into the Army. She said, "They are drafting the men who were discharged as fast they get home."

The next day I called Lieutenant Commander Gusparidge.

I told him, "I will stay in the Navy, but I will not ship over." He said, "That is fine. Just come on back as soon as your leave is over." I informed the rest of the men in my salvage team that were awaiting processing for discharge from the United States Navy what I had learned. I told them, "Men being discharged from the Navy are being drafted into the Army as soon as they return home. I plan to stay in the Navy to avoid the draft until the end of the Korean conflict, and I am going to work for Lieutenant Commander Gusparidge." When members of my salvage crew realized that they would be drafted into the Army upon their discharge from the Navy, they also decided to stay in the Navy and to work for Lieutenant Commander Gusparidge. I passed onto my salvage crew that once they completed their leave to report back to San Diego. In San Diego, we would help Lieutenant Commander Gusparidge outfit the ship that we would be taking into the Korean conflict. Lieutenant Commander Gusparidge had told us to put on our leave papers to report to the USS Jefferson County LST 845 at the conclusion of our leave. I had heard of the USS Jefferson County. This ship had started service as a tank landing ship following her commissioning in January, 1945. Prior to going on leave, I had the recruitment and discharge center prepare a document. This special document stated I was staying in the United States Navy until the end of the Korean conflict.

When my leave ended, I reported back to the Naval Base at San Diego. Upon reporting in, I asked the duty officer about the status of the USS Jefferson County. He said, "The USS Jefferson County is still in the Navy ship yards on Mare Island." I said, "Are you sure about that?" He said, "yes." I said, "It has not gone overseas." He responded, "No." Mare Island is the name for a peninsula that runs next to the city of Vallejo, California, that is about twenty-three miles northeast of San Francisco, California. The duty officer arranged for a flight for me and my crew to Alameda field. From Alameda field, we caught a ride over to

Mare Island. I went in and reported to Lieutenant Commander Gusparidge. I asked Lieutenant Commander Gusparidge, "What do you need me to do?" He said, "We are trying to get LST 845 ready to go. You will be in charge of the main engine room, and you will have Cornwell and Hill working for you. Fisher will be in charge of the auxiliary engine room, and he will have Barringer and Peters working for him." He went on to name the placement of the remainder of my salvage team on the ship. In addition, he indicated that I would be second in command of the small boats and landing craft.

When I became a part of the crew of the USS Jefferson County, I was a Third Class Petty Officer, and of the mandatory Navy duties, I had not been assigned compartment cleaning. Lieutenant Commander Gusparidge, had told me, "Red, since you are a Third Class Petty Officer, you do not have to do compartment cleaning, unless you want to." However, I had read the Articles for the Government of the Navy, better-known as "Rocks and Shoals," which stated that I was required to complete compartment training and to have the appropriate entry made in my service record book. I looked my new Skipper square in the eyes and said, "I will complete my compartment cleaning training as required by Rocks and Shoals." So for one month, I was tasked with compartment cleaning along with my regular engineering duties on the USS Jefferson County.

The smooth and efficient manner in which I handled compartment cleaning made others on the ship want the duty of compartment cleaning. For me, compartment cleaning consisted of cleaning the living quarters of the engineering section, cleaning the engineering section's head, and doing the engineering section's laundry. To accomplish these tasks, I set up a procedure. First, clean the laundry, second, dust and sweep the floors, and finally, clean the heads. In the heads, someone had painted all the brass work, and it looked terrible. So I took one head at a time and stripped the paint off of the brass work. When I finished cleaning, buffing, and polishing the brass work, the engineering section had the best looking heads on the USS Jefferson County. A few days later I located a ship that I had salvaged a few months earlier, which had mirrors, that was going to be transferred to the Japanese government. So, I removed the mirrors from this ship and installed them in the heads in the engineering section. After this, it was not long until all the sections wanted mirrors in their heads too!

The LST 845 was a rust bucket, when I started working on it, but I made it sea worthy before we sailed for Korea. We transformed the LST 845 from a floating piece of scrap metal into a real warship. My engineering section worked constantly to improve this LST. We put twenty caliber and forty caliber guns on the USS Jefferson County even though it did not rate these weapons. My efforts to arm this LST had intensified because I knew that our ship would be involved in making the troop landings for the Korean conflict. At mid-ship, my engineering section installed twin 20 caliber machine guns (one on each side). On each side of the bow, we put 40 caliber machine guns. We put 40 caliber machine guns on each side of the quarter deck and a 40 caliber machine gun on the stern.

My engineering section and I re-piped, re-wired, and re-painted the entire ship. I also had all the dogging arms on the doors, valve handles, spigot handles, knobs, and pipes on the engines chromed. I knew that it would only take a couple of minutes for these items to be chromed if placed in the molten chrome. Petty Officer Jones ran the Navy metallization shop on Marianna Island, which did the galvanizing and chrome work. While Petty Officer Jones was busy, I lowered the package of items from LST 845 into the molten chrome chamber. When Petty Officer Jones finally realized what I had done, he came running over saying, "You cannot do that." I responded, "Sorry." I pulled the items that I had lowered into the molten chrome back to the surface. It was a "fait accompli." In other words, there was nothing anyone could do about it since these items were now chromed. In addition, I took all the engineering deck plates of the USS Jefferson County to the Naval yards where I had friends. With the help of these friends who turned a blind eye to what I was doing, I got these items galvanized.

On the same day that I reported to the USS Jefferson County, I went down to look at the main and auxiliary engine rooms. In the auxiliary engine room, I met a sailor named Kirk from Little Rock, Arkansas. I was shocked, when I saw all the naked wires, plugs, and exposed switches. During a quick walk through of the main engine room, I noticed the same. There were many naked wires, unprotected wiring panels, and switches dangling in the air. All of these wiring hazards would make working in the main engine room and auxiliary engine room very dangerous. I told Kirk, "These engine rooms are very dangerous places." Kirk said, "What are you going to do?" I turned to Kirk and said, "I am going to fix it."

To correct these problems, I needed several sheets of Bakelite. Bakelite is the trademark term used to refer to a plastic material used as insulation to cover-up exposed wiring. The Bakelite came in a sheet four feet by eight feet by one-fourth of an inch in thickness. I would use the Bakelite as the surface to properly mount the dangling switches and to shield sailors from accidently falling into uncovered electrical and junction boxes. I also needed sheets of Bakelite to set up panel boards with breakers in both the auxiliary and main engine rooms. Obtaining these sheets of Bakelite required a bit of deception by the sailors in my engineering section and me. We called obtaining the materials we needed to fix the ship "comshaw" or "midnight short stories." Comshaw was a slang term used by sailors referring to the Naval practice of removing United States Government property without permission to use for one's own ship or unit. The United States Navy had warehouses full of materials such as Bakelite, which we needed to make the USS

Jefferson County safe and functional. The problem was that we had to get access to these stockpiled materials. Normally, to obtain an item from a Navy Supply Depot, we had to turn in a broken widget to receive a new widget, or we had to have a signed requisition authorizing us to obtain the item we sought. Since the LST we were on was designed to make only one voyage across the ocean, the supply personnel and comptroller were not keen on spending money to fix our LST or to make it safe for the sailors or troops being transported. To work around this problem, I had a young man in my engineering section by the name of Lenin who was forced to join the United States Navy because of forgery. I would have Lenin prepare requisition forms for the items that we needed. We would find out who the officer was that would be required to approve our requisitions. We would then have Lenin forge his name onto our requisitions. Next, we would hand our forged requisitions to the individuals operating the Navy supply warehouse and load up the equipment and supplies being requisitioned. After we had gotten the supplies and equipment, I would send Ashley, a sailor in my engineering section, to steal our requisition forms back. Ashley was an incredible pick pocket. He was so good that he could take the watch off your arm, and you would never miss it. In fact, Ashley could steal the belt right out of your pants. Like Lenin, Ashley had opted to go into the United States Navy rather than the penitentiary for being a pick pocket.

The way I looked at our comshaw operation was that all of the equipment and supplies were still in the United States Navy just in a different location. For example, on our ship, we did not have any washing machines, ironing boards, presses, or dryers. However, it was not long before my engineering section and I had obtained these items through comshaw.

Because of all the repairs being made to LST 845, special ship engineers came aboard to inspect the ship. Since this was a special inspection, it occurred after LST 845 had departed the Navy ship yards at Mare Island. These inspectors were impressed by the changes and improvements that had been made. Overall the ship received outstanding marks in all but one area, the safety lines for the small boats. To fix this problem my engineering section rigged new safety lines. The new lines were tied off to a half inch cable that was spliced between the boat davit arms. The well deck of each boat had three safety lines, and one additional safety line was located at the coxswain cubicle. The well deck of a small boat can best be described as an exposed deck lower than decks fore and aft. By regulation, each of the safety lines for the small boat was fifteen feet long. The theory was that each crew member of the small boat and coxswain would hold on to the safety line when the small boat was being lowered or raised by the ship davits. The davits of a Navy ship are crane-like devices used for supporting, raising, and lowering boats from a dry berthing to the water's surface. By holding onto the safety line, your life would be saved if something happened that caused the boat to fall. After all the safety lines were in place, the inspectors came back to check them. Outstanding marks on the installation of the safety lines were received.

A week later my small boat was being lowered into the water by the davits when the front break away connector malfunctioned. This caused the bow of the small boat to break loose and fall into the water. Unlucky for me, I was holding the safety line like I was supposed to when the small boat crashed bow first into the water. The other three crew members who were in the well deck of the boat were not holding the safety lines. Everything happened so fast it was hard to sort out the chain of events. Bottom-line, I was hanging out over the ocean. However, I could not drop into the water for fear of hitting the small boat. A backup small boat was lowered to help disconnect the first small boat that was hung up. While all this was going on, I was still hanging onto the safety line in the air. The boat davits were reversed, which brought them back aboard. Now I was hanging twenty-five feet above the steel main deck, and I could not drop onto it. From my perspective, the safety line was a disaster. With the davits over the main deck, there was only one thing I could do. I had to climb up the safety line to the half inch cable, swing hand over hand to the location where the cable attached to the davit arm, and pull myself up onto the davit arm. The davit arm was a rectangular piece of steel ten feet by six inches by twelve inches. I shimmied over the davit arm to the main part of the davit. Next, I bear hugged the main davit, and I eased myself down until I reached the rungs of the service ladder, which ran up the side of the davit from the main deck. Once I got down, I never used the safety line again.

My crew and I also picked up a hot water heater so that we could have hot fresh water showers aboard the ship. We obtained the hot water heater in Seattle, Washington, when the USS Jefferson County was on its shake-down cruise. The hot water heater was sitting on the end of a pier in Seattle so we borrowed it. Picking up this hot water heater was a well timed operation. I had a member of my crew hook-up a rig to the heater for lifting by a crane. I moved the crane on the LST 845 in position. As our ship passed the pier, the heater was hooked-up, and I swung it aboard. Once the hot water heater was aboard, I realized that we could not get it down into the hold unless we cut a hole. I had my engineering section cut a hole in the side of the ship so that we could get the hot water heater below deck where it was needed. After getting the hot water heater in place, we hooked it up, but I soon discovered that we needed a circulating pump. I located a new circulating pump on another ship, which weighed about twenty-five pounds. I managed to go aboard this ship and pick up the circulating pump, but there was no way I could walk down the gangway of this ship without being seen. So I went over the side of the ship with the pump. I swam about two hundred yards with the twenty-five pound circulating pump in my arms. When I reached the berthing pier for LST 845, I came up the gangway carrying the new circulating pump. With all these parts, I was able to install the hot water heater and to re-pipe the showers so that all the showers aboard the LST were hot fresh water showers. Until I worked on this LST, no one had tried to make this ship more habitable. My goal was to make life aboard this LST bearable. The LST is an amazing ship. It had a maximum speed of about 10 knots per hour. However, with a flat bottom, the LST did not take waves very well. It could carry 25 tanks in the cargo hold, and it could haul enough fuel, water, and food for its crew to sail around the world.

When we received orders to go to Korea, the USS Jefferson County was required to stand a readiness inspection. The inspectors came on board. When they walked into the main engine room, that was as far as they went. The inspectors were so amazed at the way that I had set up the engine room that they did not even bother to inspect the remainder of the ship. For example, before I took over the main engine room, if you were going to put water into the engines, you had to take a bucket over to the tap, fill the bucket with water, carry it to the engine, take off the radiator cap, and pour it into the engine. What I did was run a pipe from the water line up over the ceiling and down to the engines, put a drop leg into each engine, and soldered a nipple into the end of the pipe with a valve. Then, if a member of my engineering section or I came by and saw that an engine needed water, it could be filled by simply turning on the valve, filling it, and replacing the radiator cap. Furthermore, the deck plates in the engine room, instead of being the old red lead painted deck plates, I had galvanized them, and boy did they shine! All the engine pipes were chromed. In short, the auxiliary engine room and the main engine room looked fantastic. The engines in the auxiliary and main engine rooms looked more like the engines one would see in a race car.

Through my comshaw efforts, I had obtained a degaussing

unit for the USS Jefferson County. A degaussing unit is used to decrease, eliminate, or neutralize the magnetic field around a ship. By removing a ship's magnetic field, a degaussing unit could prevent torpedoes and mines, which operated off of magnetic attraction from being attracted to the ship.

When I tested the small boats on the USS Jefferson County, I discovered that less than half of them would even float. But I corrected this problem right after the first landing in Korea. The first landing like all of the subsequent landings found numerous small boats beached because of careless or incompetent boat operators. I took the unseaworthy small boats on the USS Jefferson County and traded them for the good ones we found grounded on the beaches. Swapping small boats was a simple matter. We simply painted our serial number on the beached boat and painted the serial number of the beach boat on the unseaworthy boat, which we were leaving behind. When we were finished, no one could prove that the new small boat did not belong to our LST. I had a sailor in my engineering section who was an artist. In less than 15 minutes he could switch the serial numbers of the two small boats. With this kind of speed in swapping small boats, I was able to replace all of our LST's unseaworthy small boats after the first landing in Korea. I was able to accomplish these comshaw and midnight small stories because my crew and I knew what we needed! If there were items, which our ship required, left abandoned anywhere, those items were ours. Perhaps the thing that made our activities to recover beached small boats or the comshaw of items from the Navy Supply Depot so easy was the fact that my entire salvage crew was with me on this LST. My engineering section on the USS Jefferson County was made up of my salvage team, and it was probably the best and most efficient in the United States Navy. The USS Jefferson County was the only LST to ever get the E for efficiency in the Navy's Seventh Fleet. Furthermore, outside of my salvage team, there were very few experienced small boat operators in the entire Seventh Fleet. After World War II, complacency had occurred in many areas of the United States Navy. World War II had been the war to end all wars. One of the areas where the Navy became very complacent was in the training of small boat operators.

CHAPTER 14
KOREAN WAR

As a standing order at the start of the Korean War, all officers and noncommissioned officers were required to attend a course on first aid. Documentation for attendance of the first aid class was required to be placed in our service record books before we could depart for a Korean War mission. On the USS Jefferson County, my first aid class was very interesting. The first thing that the instructors taught us was how to assist in the birth of a child. To me, this seemed ridiculous. I thought to myself, "I will never need to know how to help with the birth of a child." Prior to this training, all I had ever heard was that you were supposed to boil water. In fact, boiling water had nothing to do with birthing a baby. After this training, I informed my small boat crew and the sailors in my engineering section on how to help with the birth of a child. My boat crew and the sailors in the engineering section got a big laugh out of the child birthing information. Many of these same sailors had worked for me as part of my salvage crew. We had been together for sometime so this information about the birth of a child really seemed funny. However, the first thing that happened, during one of the withdrawals that we made in Korea, involved a Korean woman who ran up the bow ramp of the boat screaming. About that time, the bow hook, John Bousarge, started yelling, "For Christ's sake, Red you better get over here. There is something wrong with this lady!" I yelled back to John Bousarge, "For Christ's sake, what's the matter with her?" He responded, "I do not know, but I think she is calving." I told Bousarge, "You are supposed to take care of the child birth." John Bousarge turned to me and said, "No, I did not go through the training." I looked at the Korean woman and the child's head had already started to come out. I told John Bousarge, "Throw me one of the foul weather jackets." The woman was about to give birth right on the steel deck. About that time the baby popped out and I had a bloody mess and baby in my hands. I took the foul weather jacket and wrapped the baby in it. The next problem was the umbilical cord connecting the baby and the mother. In the first aid training, the instructors had emphasized tying off the umbilical cord on each end with a string. The only string that I had was my shoe lace that I took out of my shoe. I cut my shoe lace in half and tied it off next to the baby and next to the woman and cut between them. By tying them off when you cut the umbilical cord, neither the baby nor the mother bleed to death. This is the primary step to be taken before severing the umbilical cord. After tying the umbilical cord off, I took my pocket knife and severed the umbilical cord. Helping with the birth of a child is not something I ever wanted to do, but because of the fact that we were in the thick of battle, I had no choice. If I had been given a choice, I would desire to be somewhere else rather than helping with the birth of a child.

At the start of the Korean War, the North Korean forces consisted of North Koreans with Russian advisors. No Chinese or Chinese advisors were involved at this time. The North Koreans pushed the South Koreans all the way to Pusan. Pusan is a port city located in the extreme southern part of Korea. The United States had a large number of military personnel in southern Korea who helped stop the North Korean advance and pushed the North Koreans back North of the 38th parallel. President Truman declared the Korean conflict to be a police action, and the United States began preparing for an expected future assault that would combine the North Korean and Chinese forces.

When General MacArthur started work on his plan for the Inchon landing, the United States Navy started checking on how many experienced small boat operators were in the Navy. In the whole Seventh Fleet there were seven small boat operators. Most of the small boat operators had gotten out of the United States Navy after World War II, and the Navy had not trained replacements. Of the seven small boat operators in the Seventh Fleet, three of them were on the LST 845 commanded by Lieutenant Commander Gusparidge. There was me and two other members of my old salvage crew. The three of us from LST 845 were sent to Tokyo, Japan, to set up a small boat school to train small boat operators. Our job was to train as many small boat operators as quickly as possible in preparation for the Inchon landing to be made in Korea. To give my students realistic training on the handling of a small boat, I would take my students out on the small boats to the mud flats outside of Tokyo Harbor. It was hilarious to watch the students turn the small boats sideways to the ground swells vice perpendicular to the ground swells. The students would do the unexpected resulting in getting stuck on the beach or capsized. I explained to my students that operating a small boat is like operating a car. In the classroom, I could tell my students what to do, but it would go in one ear and come out the other. Until the students got in the small boats and experienced it themselves, they did not understand what I was talking about. After the students experienced driving the small boats, they could relate and understood what I had said. Experience is a great teacher. Most of the students, after getting stuck or capsized finally learned what they needed to do. I trained small boat operators from the middle of July until the middle of August 1950. While I was training small boat operators, the USS Jefferson County had sailed to Fort Lewis, Washington, to pick up supplies, fuel, and equipment. Then, the USS Jefferson County sailed down the west coast of the United States to pick up United States Marines for the upcoming landing being planned by General MacArthur.

When I re-joined the USS Jefferson County in San Diego, California, there were four Third Class Engineer Petty Officers on board. Those four were Fisher, Peters, Coburn, and me. The only advantage that I had over the other Third Class Engineer Petty Officers on the ship was that I had been a salvage crew leader. Lieutenant Commander Gusparidge called me up to the bridge and said, "I am going to make you the Engineering Officer for the ship." One of the drawbacks to being an Engineering Officer was that you had to do a great deal of typing. All the reports from the engineering section had to be typed. Typing all the engineer reports almost drove me crazy. All the reports had to be perfect with no errors.

On the USS Jefferson County, a sailor by the name of John Trevel from Memphis, Tennessee, wanted to transfer to the engineering section. Seaman Trevel stated that he wanted to learn about the engineering section, how to operate a small boat, and to do on the job training to obtain a new military occupational specialty. Because we were short sailors in the engineering section, I approved Seaman Trevel's transfer to the engineering section. Seaman Trevel was a yeoman. I was probably the first Engineering Officer to have my own yeoman. A yeoman is a clerk typist who handles administrative paperwork. True to my word, I taught John Trevel how to operate a small boat. In fact, John Trevel became one of the best small boat operators on the ship. From the time that we left the United States no one had bothered to type up the engineering log. So we had a pile of typing that needed to be done, and John

Trevel was an outstanding typist. I never would have gotten all of these reports typed if it had not been for John Trevel. In fact, I probably would have been able to retire from the Navy before I had typed all of these engineering log reports.

On the 23rd day of August, 1950, we left southern California for Korea, where we eventually joined Task Force 90. Task Force 90 consisted of a hodgepodge of different ships transporting United States forces to Korea. Within Task Force 90, there were 37 World War II vintage LSTs. Task Force 90 commanded by Vice Admiral Struble sailed up the west coast of Korea to a place off the coast from Inchon.

For months General MacArthur had been planning an invasion of Korea at Inchon to relieve the besieged Pusan perimeter. The tide fluctuations at Inchon were incredible. The Inchon tide ranged as much as thirty-two feet. These tidal fluctuations were among the greatest in the world. Because of these tremendous tidal changes, there were very few dates that the tide would be high enough to allow the amphibious ship's landing craft the time needed to conduct an amphibious landing at Inchon. Once the tides went out, the coast around Inchon became an impassible quagmire of mud.

Just before dawn on the 15th of September 1950, my small boat crew and I started landing Marines at Red Beach on Wolmi-Do Island. Before we could land forces at Inchon, it was necessary to seize control of the off-shore island, Wolmi-Do. Neutralizing Wolmi-Do Island removed the element of surprise because it took 11 hours before Marine forces could move past this island, which commanded the approaches to Inchon. Aside from Wolmi-Do, the beachhead at Inchon had other drawbacks: the steep hills ashore provided an excellent vantage point from which the enemy could rain devastating fire onto the landing force; there was no place for heavy cargo-handling; and no main roads for movement of the force once ashore.

Just before sunset on the 15th of September my crew and

I started landing Marines on Blue Beach at Inchon. For each of these landings, I was a coxswain, and my small boat was the leader carrying the flag. All the other small boat operators would follow me into the landing site. When I took the first wave of landing craft to the Blue Beach, I was shocked to see what the North Koreans had done. All along the rock walls and boulders at the beachhead, the North Koreans had chained their soldiers so they could not run. Some of the North Koreans were chained by the wrist and others were chained by the foot. The result was the North Korean soldiers along the beachheads at Inchon could not leave. These North Korean soldiers had no choice but to stay and fight. When the large LSTs pulled up to the shore to unload the heavy equipment and tanks, many lowered the bow door on these North Korean soldiers who were chained to rocks or in bunkers along the beachhead. The bow doors simply crushed the North Korean soldiers who were chained to their positions. None of the Commanders of the LSTs intentionally lowered the bow door on chained North Korean soldiers. It was only after daybreak and the bow doors were raised that the crushed, chained North Korean soldiers were discovered along the rock walls and bunkers on the beachhead. The two Marine regiments that we landed at Inchon climbed over sea walls and other North Korean barriers, and within a matter of hours, these Marines had destroyed or captured the North Korean troops defending the city.

As part of the supporting second wave, I helped transport a unit from the Army National Guard. We landed the Army reserve unit out of Nashville, Tennessee on the beachhead in Inchon. This Army National Guard was associated with the Grand Ole Opry. All the way from Japan to Korea, they played country music.

Earlier in the day my boat crew and I had been running non-stop to land the Marines on the beachheads from the different LSTs in Task Force 90. As evening approached, my crew and I started running the Landing Craft Mechanized (LCM), which was designed for carrying vehicles and supplies. We called the LCMs, "M boats." The M boats came to prominence during the Second World War when they were used to land tanks during Allied amphibious assaults.

As part of the preparation for a landing, the small boats are assigned different segments of the beach for landing a particular force. The normal way of designating this location is by a color. I was assigned to land my forces at Wolmi-do Island on Red Beach, and the Marines for Inchon along the strip of beachhead about 200 yards wide known as Blue Beach. I was driving the flag boat for the landing. The flag boat operator is the leader of the landing boat wave. To designate my small boat as the flag landing boat, a flag had been placed to wave above my small boat. All other boat operators followed my lead. I did not like being the flag boat because that made you the prime target for the enemy. As the flag boat operator, you were always the first boat to drop troops ashore. You also were the leader, which circled the small boats offshore to get them lined up to make the rush to the assigned beach. During the landing at Inchon, my small boat and the others worked as long as we could until the tide went out. When the tide started going out, I tied up my boat to the stern of the LST 845 so my crew and I could climb aboard. My crew and I had not eaten since the night before, and it was after 2:00 P.M. I wanted to get some food for my crew so that we would be ready when the tide came back in. All around us there were shells exploding and bullets being fired. I knew the tide was going out, but I never thought that all of the water would go out. All of a sudden the LST we were on listed over on its side. I got my crew and we went back to the small boat, but there was no place to run it. You cannot run a small boat in mud. It requires water too. I looked back towards Wolmi-Do, and you could not even see the water. Our LST was sitting right in the middle of a mud flat.

While my crew and I were sitting on the deck of the LST, we looked up at the sky. There was a dogfight taking place between a United States jet fighter and a North Korean jet fighter. The way the dogfight was going, I thought the North Korean was going to shoot the American down. The North Korean aircraft appeared to be more maneuverable. If I had been a gambling man, I would have bet that the North Korean was going to shoot down the American. To avoid being shot down, the American suddenly went into a steep dive right at the mud flat. Instead of trying to pull the aircraft upright, like I would have, the American pilot came back in under himself and up. You could see the mud fly from the American's jet engines as he went through this maneuver. The American jet came within twenty feet of the ground as he went upside down back up into the air. The North Korean who was trailing the American could not maneuver fast enough to avoid slamming into the mud flat. The North Korean jet fighter was buried in the mud all the way up to the tail. There were a great many pictures taken of this North Korean jet fighter buried in the mud all the way up to his tail. I did not take a picture because I did not even own a camera at the time.

One of the most costly battles was fought over the island called Wolmi-Do. This was the landing that we made just prior to the landing at Inchon, Korea. The battle for Wolmi-Do cost a great many Marine lives. During the Korean War, almost all amphibious operations were made by Marines. This was true of Wolmi-Do Island. We landed about two thousand Marines on Wolmi-Do at daylight on September 15. By 9:00 A.M., the Marines had run to the top of Wolmi-Do Island and put the United Sates flag up. The Marines had fought all the way to the top killing large numbers of North Koreans. During the remainder of the day, we landed Marines and supplies at the Inchon beachheads. About an hour after sunset, General Quarters sounded on the announcer of LST 845. Lieutenant Commander Gusparidge screamed into the announcer, "All boats away, the Marines are being overrun on Wolmi-Do." My crew and I led the small boats over to Wolmi-Do to pickup the Marines who were fighting their way back down to the beach. It seemed like this same scenario occurred every day for a week. My crew and I got to the point where we could make the landing and pickup on Wolmi-Do Island in our sleep. I look back on this as a tremendous tragedy because of the large number of Marine lives lost trying to secure this island. No one could figure out where all the North Koreans were coming from that kept attacking the Marines each night.

Finally, after a week of landing the Marines and evacuating them, we stopped. A few days later, a troop transport arrived with a United States Army unit aboard. The next day my crew and I landed this United States infantry unit. At this point, I did not have much faith that American forces would be able to take and hold this island. I certainly did not think that this unit could take Wolmi-Do. We completed the landing of the Army infantry unit around noon. Lieutenant Commander Gusparidge called me back to the ship after the landing to eat lunch and to get ready for an expected evacuation that night. Later that afternoon, we lowered the small boats to resume hauling supplies and ammo ashore. With the Marines the United States flag was normally flying over Wolmi-Do by 9:00 A.M. Unlike the Marines, the United States Army had not moved off the beach. We had to clear the Army out of the way so that we could let the ramp down on the boat. The next day we carried the Army unit more supplies. We could still see the Army unit from the boat. The Army infantry had moved about 100 yards inland from the day before. In effect, the Army infantry dug foxholes from the bottom of Wolmi-Do to the top about every 100 yards. It took the Army infantry about three weeks to make it to the top of Wolmi-Do, but when this Army unit made it to the top, the island was secure. This made an impression on me. If you wanted a force to sit and hold a location, you wanted the

United States Army infantry. During the methodical process of digging foxholes to the top of Wolmi-Do, the Army infantry had discovered the cave, which the North Koreans were using at low tide to funnel large numbers of troops onto Wolmi-Do Island. The Marines had been continuously overrun by the North Koreans because of the huge numbers of troops being run through this cave. When the tide would go out in the evening, the North Koreans could walk from mainland Korea through the cave. The Marines did not find the cave, but the Army did because of their methodical advance and foxhole digging. The Army Infantry unit never got in a hurry, and we continued to haul ammunition and stack it on the beach for the Army.

A week later, I learned that two sailors from our ship had jumped ship (unauthorized absence) and gone to Seoul, Korea. Both of these sailors were part of the deck crew. These sailors were going to help the Marines fight the North Koreans. After the landing at Inchon, I had participated in all the Korean War that I wanted. I was ready to go back to Japan to watch the Geisha women. However, Lieutenant Commander Gusparidge volunteered Fisher and me to go get the two sailors who had jumped ship. The roads from Inchon to Seoul were non-existent. I thought we would never make it to Seoul. I said to myself, "Here is a country older than Christ, and they do not even have any roads." Fisher and I tried to obtain directions from the Korean farmers along the way, but we could not speak Korean, and the Koreans could not speak English. When we would speak to a Korean, we would say, "Can you point us in the direction of Seoul?" and the Korean would respond, "Ah so, Ah so." I would look at Fisher and say, "Do you know what he said?" Fisher would laugh, and we would go on to the next Korean and ask him "Where is Seoul?" Finally, with a little luck, we made it to Seoul. The Marine Corps unit, which the sailors tried to join, had captured the sailors and were holding them in a make shift brig. After picking up these two sailors, we made our way back to our ship. The trip to pickup these two sailors took about three days, but it should have taken about three hours. If there had been a road, it would not have taken three hours. Upon our return to LST 845, we started preparations for the next landing. Because of all the landings that I participated in, I received a ribbon denoting 3 battle stars and 3 beachheads for the Korean conflict. My boat crew and I made every amphibious landing and every withdraw on the Korean peninsula.

Once the reinforcements had landed at Inchon, the North Koreans fled to the North. Many of the Korean soldiers appeared to me to be fighting for which ever side was feeding them. Some Korean units changed sides just like you or I would change socks. It appeared unclear to me whether they were North or South Koreans. What seemed to be the determining factor was who was feeding them. I would take a boat load of the North Korean prisoners out to an island where the United Nations had established an enemy prisoner of war camp. A month later, I would pick up a load of Koreans from the enemy prisoner of war camp and take them to a location to make a landing. I thought this was a very dumb way to fight a war.

The landings at Wolmi-Do and Inchon were considered overwhelming successes. Vice Admiral Struble had turned over direct oversight of these landings to the brilliant amphibious force commander, Rear Admiral Doyle, who masterfully executed the amphibious landings at Wolmi-Do and Inchon.

After the landings at Wolmi-Do and Inchon, we traveled to Kobe, Japan. Kobe is the fifth largest city in Japan, and it is located on the southern side of the main island of Honshu about nineteen miles west of Osaka. In Kobe, LST 845 had been ordered to resupply and to pick up a thousand Marines and their equipment for a new landing in Korea. This new landing was being planned for a place called Wonsan. General Douglas MacArthur had ordered X Corps, which included First Marine Division, to make the landing at Wonsan. X Corp and

First Marine Division were to proceed west to link up with the Eighth Army. Then both would advance towards Pyongyang, the capital of North Korea. The landing at Wonsan faced one major problem. North Korean naval forces had been well supplied by the Soviet Union and China with all sorts of sea mines. These mines had been strategically placed in mine fields within Wonsan Harbor. This made an amphibious assault through the harbor almost impossible. To overcome this obstacle, the Navy had to identify and to plot the location of the mine fields within Wonsan Harbor. Next, the mine fields had to be destroyed. Operation Wonsan began during the first part of October, 1950. Rear Admiral Doyle who had assumed command of Task Force 90 was given the responsibility of neutralizing the Wonsan Harbor mine fields.

To gain additional intelligence for the Wonsan Harbor landing, several Marine Corps reconnaissance teams had been sent ashore. My boat crew and I were sent to pick up one of the reconnaissance teams. This reconnaissance team was led by a Second Lieutenant. We were to pick up his team on the north side of Wonsan Harbor. Along the north side of the harbor, a rock sea wall had been built to keep the high tide from swamping the town of Wonsan, which was located three miles further up the harbor. This rock wall extended out into the harbor about a mile. My boat crew and I made it into Wonsan Harbor, and we located the Second Lieutenant's reconnaissance team. After we got his reconnaissance team and their equipment on board, a North Korean fighter attacked. Luckily, my boat was underway when the North Korean fighter attempted his strafing run. I did a couple of quick maneuvers, and the North Korean fighter missed us completely. During this maneuvering, the Second Lieutenant had jumped up and said, "I order you to surrender." In response, I told Bousarge, "Kill him if he gets up in my face again." Everyone on the boat was frightened. As I came out of one of my turns, I pulled up in a cove twenty feet from land, and

I asked, "Does anyone want to get off because I intend to run the mine field?" No one wanted to get off so I came out of the cove and headed towards the mine field. There were two Korean warships tied off in the channel about twenty-five feet apart. The deck guns on both Korean warships were firing at us. As I turned toward the Korean warships, I was running about two thirds speed. I cranked it up to flank speed, and I jumped the governors on the two big diesel engines. When I went between the two warships, my boat was going so fast that it was standing up. Only the stern engine propellers were in the water with the bow up in the air. The boat was going in excess of thirty-five knots as we hit the mine field. This mine field was about a mile wide. Suddenly, we heard an explosion back behind us. A North Korean gunboat had tried to follow us. When the North Korean gunboat came through the gap between the two warships, it ran head-on into a floating mine that popped to the surface in our wake. We went across the mine field at flank speed without any trouble. The key to crossing the mine field was to avoid hitting a mine that was just barely under the water's surface or one that was floating on the surface. We were moving so fast that the magnetic mines could not break lose from their moorings fast enough to hit us. I was standing on the gunwale of the boat so that I could see the water in front of the boat to avoid a collision with a mine on the surface or one just under the water's surface.

When we got back to LST 845, I had not finished my report when I was directed by the Master at Arms to the ward room. The ward room on LST 845 was the area that served as the living quarters for all the ship's officers, except the commanding officer. It also included a dining area and a lounge for these officers. When I arrived at the ward room, I explained to Lieutenant Commander Gusparidge that I had not finished my report yet. At that point, Lieutenant Commander Gusparidge replied, "The Second Lieutenant has filed charges against you."

Standing with the Lieutenant Commander was an Admiral. This Admiral asked me, "Did you order a man to kill the Second Lieutenant?" I replied, "Yes sir, I ordered Bousarge to kill the Second Lieutenant if he got up in my face again." I explained that the Second Lieutenant had ordered me to surrender, and that I had pulled up near the shore where those who wanted to leave the landing craft and surrender could wade ashore. No one indicated that they wanted off, so we came between the two Korean warships blocking the channel at flank speed into the mine field.

After I told Lieutenant Commander Gusparidge and the Admiral what had happened, the Admiral asked the Second Lieutenant, "Did you ask permission to come aboard the landing craft?" The Second Lieutenant replied, "No sir, I did not." The Admiral then explained that when the Second Lieutenant came aboard, the man in charge of the boat is the Captain. He told the Second Lieutenant, "You have no authority except that which the Captain grants you." Furthermore, he told the Second Lieutenant, "You must be courteous to the Captain of the boat at all times, you must ask to come aboard, you must salute the flag, and you must salute the man in charge of the vessel." The Admiral concluded by saying, "Petty Officer Duncan showed great restraint by not having you shot!"

A few days later, we got orders to go back into Wonsan Harbor to pick up another Marine Corps reconnaissance team. We went in without any trouble, but when we got our load, a North Korean gunboat was coming straight for us. I took off because I felt that I could easily out run him and get into the open water. However, when we came around the bend in the cove, the North Koreans had moved a cargo ship crossways in the channel to block my exit from the harbor. Since the channel was blocked, I started looking for another way out. It was about 30 minutes until high tide. We circled the harbor. There was no other way out. We came around the sea wall, and I made up my mind to jump the sea wall at high tide. I told the Marines on the boat what I intended to do, and I told them that I would let them off if they wanted to surrender. Everyone wanted to stay on the boat, so at high tide I got the boat going as fast as it would go toward the sea wall. I told everyone, "Hang on to something and get down low." The crew was hanging onto the engines. The Marines were hanging on to what they could in the well deck, and I was running at flank speed towards the sea wall. When the bow cleared the wall, I cut the engine speed. We sailed over the wall into open sea. The sea wall tore the rudder off and warped the propellers, but we were out of the harbor. Luckily, no one gave chase, and we made it back to the ship. The ride back to the ship was painful. The only way I could steer the landing craft was with the propellers. Because both propellers were bent out of shape, I would turn on one propeller at a time. The bent propeller would vibrate, and the boat moved at an angle. Then I would switch engines and turn on the other propeller, which sent the boat at an angle in the other direction. Slowly, we zigzagged back to LST 845. Everyone was happy to be off the boat. The next day, we replaced the rudder and the propellers, and the boat was again ready for service.

The Army staff that had been planning the landing at Wonsan was concerned about the number of casualties that might occur from a frontal assault of the Wonsan Harbor. For this reason, several landing alternatives and strategies were being studied. One of those being studied involved Marines scaling a one hundred and fifty foot sheer rock bluff. Intelligence reported that on top of this sheer rock bluff was the Wonsan airfield. It had no heavy fortifications, and it was lightly guarded by the North Koreans. The top of the bluff was not heavily defended because no one believed that a military force could be landed there with the waves crashing into the rocks and bluff. To study this alternative, LST 845 was anchored with several Navy cargo ships about five miles outside of Wonsan Harbor. The day after we anchored, I received a message to report to the ward room. When I got to the ward room, it was full. Lieutenant Commander Gusparidge said, "Petty Officer Duncan have a seat and watch the movie. I need you to tell me if we can land troops at this location." I watched the movie, and when it was over, he asked me, "Is it possible to land troops on those rocks?" I replied, "Yes sir, I think it can be done, but I need to see the place in person." Lieutenant Commander Gusparidge said, "Get your boat ready so you can go look at the site tonight." After looking at the proposed sheer rock bluff landing site, I reported back to Lieutenant Commander Gusparidge. During this meeting, I explained to Lieutenant Commander Gusparidge that I could land the Marines in two runs. I told him that there was a small flat rock at the base of the bluff at high tide. On the first run, I would put part of the Marines off with their equipment, and on the second run, I would put the rest off. I further explained that when the Marines left the boat the weight imbalance would force the boat into the rocks where the side of the boat might be damaged or destroyed.

The very next night we went back to the sheer rock bluff just outside of Wonsan Harbor to make this landing. As I looked at the bluff, I found the flat rock that I had briefed to Lieutenant Commander Gusparidge. That rock was eight feet wide by fifteen feet. This was my landing destination. However, from prior experience, I had learned that when driving a small boat, the ocean often decided where you would land. I had about fifty Marines aboard my boat. On the first run, I landed two thirds of the platoon in fine fashion. After I made the second run to let the remaining Marines off, the weight imbalance and waves pushed me into the rocks. The rocks cut a gash about six feet long down the side of the boat. The gash was not very wide, but the water was pouring in. After maneuvering the boat out of the rocks, I moved about two hundred yards from the sheer rock bluff to see how badly we were taking on water. We were able to keep the water pumped out of the boat with the bilge pump. Using night glasses, I watched the lead Marine drive a piton spike into the sheer rock bluff and attach a carabiner to the piton. A piton is a metal spike that is driven into a crack or seam in the rock with a hammer. It acts as an anchor to protect the climber against the consequences of a fall or to assist in climbing. Pitons are equipped with a ring to which a carabiner is attached. The carabiner can best be described as an oblong metal ring with a spring clip used to attach a rope. The lead Marine steadily drove pitons and attached carabiners. In no time, he had worked his way to the top of the rock bluff. Upon reaching the top, the lead Marine tied off the rope that he had run up through the carabiners. Within minutes, the rest of the Marines were on top securing the bluff and the airfield in preparation for the landing at Wonsan Harbor. With the airfield at Wonsan secured, the strategic outlook for the Wonsan Harbor landing changed dramatically. I later learned that the Marine, who climbed this sheer rock bluff that night and made a trail for the other Marines to follow, was an American Indian from Oklahoma. After returning to the ship, we patched up the hole in the small boat and got prepared for the Wonsan Harbor landing.

During the third week of October, 1950, my ship became part of a new invasion force being assembled in Japan. LST 845 was ordered back to Yokohama, Japan, to pick up Marines for the next invasion. We loaded up a reinforced company of Marines (about 800 Marines) with their equipment. On the 18th of October, we arrived back in Korean waters and anchored about three miles off the coast of Hamnung, Korea. We were waiting for the word to make the landing. Tension was running high with anticipation. Orders came down setting the time for the invasion of Hamnung. It was decided that we would start the landing at high tide at 5:30 A.M. Without a hitch, we put the Marines ashore, and they went about their business. The Army was also landed, and the cargo ships unloaded. Base camp was set up. Everything seemed to be going well. About that time, Chinese military forces came out of nowhere. Naval gunfire was destroying whole Chinese units at a time, but the Chinese just kept coming. As one Chinese unit was blown up, the Chinese forces just closed ranks and kept marching. They over ran the Marines and the Army. We evacuated everyone and everything located on the beach, but there was not time to salvage the base with its supplies. The Chinese troops were not stopped until the LSM(R)s came along the coast and fired their rockets. The LSM(R)s did a job on the Chinese ground troops. I was ordered to stay behind with two other landing craft crews to spike the guns and destroy what was still usable.

We buried the dead from the fighting in a makeshift cemetery divided into groups as follows: United States military personnel (Navy, Marines, Army, and Air Force), other United Nations members, South Koreans, North Koreans, and Chinese. We filled multiple ditches ten feet wide by six feet deep with the dead bodies. We placed a cross at the head of each body placed in the ground.

After the dead were taken care of. We started getting rid of the land mines. For security, we mounted a 50 caliber machine gun on back of a jeep. To destroy the mines, we decided to establish a series of booby traps up and down the road. We wired the land mines together so if one went off, it would set off twenty mines at a time. We buried a few in the road, but most were wired on either side of the road to go off when one was triggered. We came back and wired the fuel depot so all we had to do was activate the trigger mechanism and the whole countryside would blow up. Next, we started spiking the guns. We had been operating in Hamnung for a week, and the Chinese had not bothered to come after us. Suddenly, they decided to come down the road. For them this was a bad choice. We had four 155 Howitzers aimed up the road. What the Howitzers did not take out, the mines did as the Chinese jumped in the ditch. The next day, in preparation for leaving, we set off the remaining booby traps and Claymore mines.

The Battle of Chosin Reservoir was a decisive battle in the Korean War. Shortly before this battle, the People's Republic of China had entered the conflict on the side of North Korea. The People's Volunteer Army (Chinese 9th Army) infiltrated the northeastern part of North Korea and surprised the United States X Corps, which included the First Marine Division at the Chosin Reservoir area. A brutal battle in freezing weather followed from the end of November through the first two weeks of December, 1950. Thirty thousand United Nation troops under the command of Major General Edward Almond were encircled by approximately sixty-seven thousand Chinese troops under the command of Song Shi-Lun. Although the Chinese troops surrounded and outnumbered the United Nations forces, the United Nations forces broke out of the encirclement. During the breakout, First Marine Division inflicted crippling losses on the Chinese. Following this engagement, X Corps and First Marine Division were evacuated through the port of Hungnam. This marked the complete withdrawal of United Nations troops from North Korea.

When the soldiers and Marines reached the port of Hungnam, they were in a bad shape. The extreme cold and sleeping on frozen ground had caused many soldiers and Marines to develop frost bite on the hands, nose, ears, and cheeks. As the soldiers and Marines arrived in Hungnam, we quickly transported them to warm ships for medical treatment. Because of all the cold weather injuries (frost bite) and malfunctioning equipment that our forces had suffered, it was thought that the North Koreans and Chinese forces might be better equipped for cold weather. To answer this question, I was selected to be part of a special reconnaissance team sent to a Chinese supply depot to bring back samples of Chinese military clothing, weapons, and equipment. I was hand picked for this special reconnaissance team due to my UDT training and because I was the best small boat operator in the Seventh Fleet. Two other sailors were selected to be part of my boat crew. As part of this team, there were ten Air Force personnel. No one wore clothing showing their rank. One older gentleman was the OIC. However, all he seemed to do was pass out C-rations that were air dropped. A C-ration is a canned, pre-cooked ration that is issued to United States military land forces when fresh food or prepared food in mess halls or field kitchens is not available. These C-rations were delivered every three days by a small engine plane. You could hear this small engine plane long before you saw it. Sometimes the supply plane came early in the morning. The next time, it came late in the evening. There was no set schedule.

We sat on the beach eating C-rations for three weeks waiting to start this mission. Then one evening we were told we were moving out. The reconnaissance team got loaded on my small boat, and I was handed a map with a small inlet marked. I drove the small boat up the coast of North Korea for about four hours and turned into the small inlet. As I examined the terrain, I picked a solid sandbar at the base of a gently sloping ridge to beach the boat. Next, we traveled by foot up the ridge line for three miles. When we arrived, Air Force personnel moved ahead to eliminate the Chinese guards. After the Chinese guards had been eliminated and the warehouses unlocked, we were signaled to move into the supply depot. Next, the OIC pulled out a list of the items to be taken. We went through the warehouses picking up the items on the list. We piled the clothing, hats, gloves, ski masks, coats, coveralls, and different types of footwear into the back of one of the small jeeps that had been selected for removal. Several different versions of jeeps with very broad tires were started and driven back to the boat. Other vehicles that we brought back included a small light weight tank, a small armored vehicle, and a dual wheeled jeep-like vehicle with tracks. By the time, I arrived back at the boat driving the dual wheeled jeep-like vehicle with tracks, an airstrike was underway by United States fighter jets against the supply depot that we had just raided. This was a top secret mission. On this mission, there were no United Nations troops along for the ride. When we got back to LST 845 with the stuff we had confiscated, everything was documented and photographed. I later heard that some of the technology that we had confiscated was incorporated into weapons, equipment, and clothing to be used by our servicemen. On this mission, the Air Force did an outstanding job. This was the only operation that I was ever on with Air Force personnel.

There were two times in Korea that I should have been killed, but by the grace of God, I was not. One incident occurred at Inchon. Our LST was on the beach. I had gone out in front of the ship on the beach to watch the war. In Korea the North Koreans and Chinese used knee mortars. When you heard the first mortar, you had better start looking for cover because the third one would be right on target (right in your back pocket). The North Koreans and Chinese were excellent with the knee mortar. I heard the first mortar coming. It fell about fifty yards in front of the ship. I started running back toward the bow door of the ship, and just as I dove into the open bow door, the third mortar hit. It threw sand all over me and the bow of the ship.

The second incident occurred outside of Hungnam. I was on special sea detail. Our ship was not at General Quarters. I had walked over to the damage control room. It was a cold but pretty day. As I stepped back out on the main deck with a head set on, the North Koreans fired a five inch round into the store room that I had just left. This round set the auxiliary engine room and the store room on fire. If I had not been outside the damage control room, where I could direct the fight against the fire, the ship might have been in peril. As it was, my damage control team was able to quickly get the fire under control. The

North Koreans had been trying to hit the fuel tanks on the LST so that the fuel would blow up. During this attack, no one from my small boat crew or engineering section was injured, but there were two of the five sailors on duty who were badly burned. They had to be evacuated. The fuel tanks of the ship were located in that section near the auxiliary engine room. The two sailors burned from the explosion were Harrington and Goodwin. Both were good friends of mine. The other three men in the auxiliary engine room and store room were able to pull the lever on the CO_2 canister. Two 500 pound bottles of CO_2 were located in the auxiliary engine room to extinguish fires. When the emergency lever on the CO_2 canister was pulled, the pressurized CO_2 filled the compartment. Since CO_2 is heavier than normal air, it immediately sank smothering the fire by cutting off its oxygen supply. Of course, the CO_2 would also smother people so once the lever was pulled everyone not dressed in protective fire fighting gear with an oxygen supply had to leave the engine room. Nothing could live in the CO_2. So the last man out of the engine room secured the engine room hatch.

Almost six months after the Korean War began, I was involved in a massive evacuation at Hungnam, Korea. Lieutenant Commander Gusparidge sent all of the small boats from LST 845 to assist with what I would describe as an amphibious operation in reverse. The evacuation at Hungnam included the bulk of United Nations forces in eastern North Korea. This was the evacuation following the Battle at Chosin Reservoir. Without question, it was the largest sealift since the 1945 Okinawa operation during World War II. Over one hundred thousand military personnel, seventeen thousand five hundred vehicles, and three hundred and fifty tons of cargo were picked up from the shore and loaded on LSTs. Unlike the retreat in central and western Korea, little was left behind. Even broken-down vehicles were loaded and lifted out. Some ninety-one thousand refugees also departed North Korea through the Hungnam evacuation.

For this evacuation, it was the refugees that posed the biggest threat. Interspersed within the refugees were North Korean fighters. These North Korean fighters were heavily armed or they had coerced a mule to carry the arms and ammunition for them. The goal of these North Korean fighters was to cause as much death, carnage, and damage as possible during the withdrawal. The refugees were the last to move toward the port to be evacuated. To reduce the impact of these North Korean fighters, Lieutenant Commander Gusparidge sent a detachment of twenty sailors with me to establish a check point to weed out the North Korean fighters from the refugees. I set up this check point 10 miles north of Hungnam along the coastal highway. For this check point, I organized my detachment into two twelve hour shifts with ten men in each shift. My initial efforts to stop the flow of small arms, hand grenades, and ammunition to Hungnam were unsuccessful. We were unsuccessful because we were only removing those weapons and munitions that were visible as the refugees came through the check point. Lieutenant Commander Gusparidge called me by radio to tell me that the small arms, hand grenades, and other munitions were still coming down the road to Hungnam. He chewed me out, and he told me, "Stop the flow of weapons to Hungnam. You have authority to use whatever you need to accomplish this task." To augment my detachment, I requested that Lieutenant Commander Gusparidge provide the following additional personnel and equipment: eight nurses who spoke Korean, six command tents, twelve 45 caliber grease guns, four Browning automatic rifles with all purpose field scopes, and a jeep load of ammunition for these weapons. Within an hour of my request, my detachment had been augmented.

Since the small arms and munitions were being smuggled down the road, I issued the order to my detachment that no one traveled down the road to Hungnam without first going through a strip search. I had two sets of three tents each put up. Each set of three tents allowed entry at the first tent and exit after moving through the first tent, through the second, and through the third tent. The refugees were divided into males and females. Females were directed through one set of tents, and the males passed through the other set of tents. Refugees were allowed to proceed one at a time into the first tent. Each refugee was met by a guard who turned them over to a nurse who spoke Korean. The nurse explained that they did not have to be strip searched unless they wanted to go on down the road to Hungnam. If they did not want to be strip searched, they could turn around and go north away from Hungnam. For those desiring to go to Hungnam, they were informed to remove any hidden ammunition, weapons, and hand grenades. It was explained to all the refugees that after they removed any hidden ammunition, weapons, and hand grenades, they would be escorted to the second tent where they would completely undress and put on a hospital gown. They would then be escorted to a third tent, where their belongings would be returned to them after being searched. Once their belongings were returned, they would be permitted to redress and continue down the road to Hungnam.

During this process, female refugees were watched by female military personnel. Men were watched and escorted by male military personnel. At my check point, seven jeep loads of small arms, hand grenades, and ammunition were collected. My detachment ran this check point for six days straight. My strip search procedure stopped the flow of weapons and ammunition. Most of the carriers or mules for smuggling the small arms, hand grenades, and ammunition were women. However, some young boys were also mules.

A few days later, while moving the LST 845 into position to make another landing along the coast of Korea, a log punctured the hull. The log made a hole about 5 inches in diameter in the bottom of the LST. Originally, the hull of the ship was made of 3/8 inch steel plate, but over the years, this LST had cycled through the process of being painted, rusting paint being chipped off, and repainted until the steel plating was probably not more than one quarter of an inch thick.

When the log jabbed through the hull, water was spraying through the hole in the hull all the way to the ceiling. It reminded me of an artesian well. Damage control was sounded. Since I was in charge of damage control, I led a team into the rapidly filling compartment to stop the leak. I had one of the members of my team grab a couple of mattresses and the other men I sent to grab a sheet of steel deck plating. The mattresses were placed over the hole and the steel deck plate on top of the mattress. Next, I had shoring material placed in position so that we could jack the mattress and steel deck plate tightly over the hole. All the circulating pumps were being used to take suction and pump the water out of the compartment. By the time, I got the leak under control, the water level had risen to waist deep in the engine room.

We were lucky because of all the electrical re-wiring that I had done on LST 845. If I had not placed all the switches up off the floor on a master switch board that I had created and if the switches had been down on the floor, we would have had to cut the power to avoid being electrocuted while stopping the leak. Cutting the power would have meant a loss of the use of the pumps, which were keeping the water from filling the compartment. The net result would have been that the ship would have sunk.

Neither the shelling of the auxiliary engine room nor the log puncturing the hull prevented our LST from completing our assigned missions. The efficiency with which my damage control team had handled both incidents resulted in a feather in the hat of our commanding officer, Gusparidge. When I got out of the Navy, Gusparidge was a full Commander. In all competitions involving our ship, we won. Our ship was the only LST that had the E for efficiency in the whole fleet. It was really unfair to the other ships in the fleet when we competed. Almost everyone on our ship had worked on my salvage crew. Most of us were also divers. Fisher and I had been through a regular engineering class, an advanced engineering school, and UDT. In addition, almost all of the other members of our crew had been through some type of engineering training.

During one of the war game drills that LST 845 participated in, the evaluator for the war game came down into the main engine room. He handed me a sheet of paper saying that the fuel pump on the Starboard engine had broken. In terms of the war game, this would have meant that our ship would have lost speed falling out of the convoy where it would have been vulnerable to submarine attack. To overcome this problem, I took a number of steps. First, I told a member of the engine room team to start manually pumping fuel for the starboard engine. I went up to the parts room, and I got a brand new fuel pump. When I returned, I had my sailors in the engineering section take the fuel pump in the line loose and remove it. Once my team pulled the fuel pump out, I spun the gears on the new pump and jammed it into the system while it was running. My crew fastened the pump down, and we didn't lose over 200 or 300 RPMs on the engine during the entire period. The game monitor was shocked by what he had seen me and my crew do when faced with an emergency. Six months after the war game, my crew and I had to demonstrate the fuel pump replacement again while the engine was running. This time the audience was comprised of all the engineering officers within Seventh Fleet and the Admiral of Seventh Fleet. No one believed that we had made this fuel pump replacement while the engine was running. However, my crew and I had made these kind of repairs and emergency maintenance numerous times.

LST 845 was assigned the mission of destroying the equipment ammo and fuel dumps being left behind at Hungnam, Korea. After the United States Army and the Marines had been evacuated, a large Chinese military force approached. Lieutenant Commander Gusparidge sent my crew ashore to insure that nothing left behind in the supply depot would fall into the hands of the Chinese military force. This was standard procedure. With my binoculars, I could see the Chinese military force coming. Our Navy gunners would blow up whole platoons and the Chinese would not even break rank. In sum, knocking out one platoon at a time had no impact on the Chinese. It was as though the Chinese soldiers were oblivious to death. This simply emphasized what I had seen earlier that the Asian nations place very little value on life, and they were very quick to sacrifice huge numbers of their soldiers for a minimal gain.

Since I knew the Chinese were trying to reach the supply depot, I decided to booby-trap the entire area. My crew and I placed five hundred claymore mines in strategic locations. I also had my engineers place whole cases of white phosphorous grenades among other ammo with booby-traps ready to go off. We had all the avenues of approach to this supply depot rigged and booby-trapped. As the Chinese tried to maneuver down to the supply depot, they ran into one booby-trap after another. It seemed that where small arms fire and naval gunfire had been ineffective to get the attention of the Chinese soldiers, the booby-traps were much more effective. The trick was to raise the stakes by increasing the carnage of the Chinese force as it approached. Hundreds of screaming Chinese on fire from white phosphorous had a very chilling effect on their advance. The bottom line was that we still held the supply depot one week later with only twenty sailors. My crew had a ball baiting the Chinese into traps and then setting them off. After several days, the Chinese decided that the supply depot was not worth the destruction of their military force. Initially, the Chinese thought that they would be able to convert the American supply depot to their own use. We quickly changed their minds about that.

It seemed that we were always going ashore after an evacuation to booby trap and spike equipment that was being left behind. Also included in this job was the very unpleasant task of burying the dead. One fellow in my burial crew was named McGoo. He would go around on the beach and knock out the gold and silver teeth from the dead and put them in a little tobacco pouch. McGoo would carry a small hammer with him to knock out the gold and silver teeth. His actions turned my stomach, but he was smarter than me because after the Korean War, he had a pretty good nest egg.

When preparing the dead on the beach, you put one dog tag between the dead military members teeth, and retain one for use to create a list of those who died. For the actual burial, bulldozers were used. The bulldozer would dig a large trench about eight to ten feet wide and one hundred yards long. The bodies being buried would be placed in the trench uniformly with the head face up all in the same direction. The bodies in the trench would be side by side with little space between each. At the head of each body, a small white cross approximately 3 feet high would be pounded into the ground. On this white cross, the dog tag would be removed from between the dead military members teeth and attached to the cross with a thumb tack. The white cross would be placed as close to the head of the dead body as possible. Next, the bulldozer would push the dirt to cover the bodies in the trench. When burying the dead great care was taken to insure uniformity, but the possibility of confusion and mix-ups involving bodies was a definite possibility. On these details my men and I did the best we could. Later, the bodies would be exhumed for re-burial in the United States or for placement in a Korean national cemetery. I remember thinking to myself that mistakes in the identification of the bodies dug-up for reburial would be common. However, under the circumstances, the hasty burials of United States military personnel and allies by my crew and me were done to the best of our ability. During these hasty burials, sporadic small arms fire was the norm, and on many occasions, the burial detail would come under sniper or mortar fire.

After the start of the Korean War, I was assigned a number of special missions. However, some missions because of the facts or circumstances were more interesting than others. On one particular mission, my small boat crew and I were tasked to go behind enemy lines to pick up a Marine Corps reconnaissance unit located well above the 38th parallel. Colonel Crowe was in charge of this Marine Corps reconnaissance unit. His unit had been landed behind enemy lines to gather intelligence information about North Korean and Chinese troop movements. On this reconnaissance operation, Colonel Crowe had two platoons (approximately one hundred Marines) with him. At the time I was assigned this mission, I had no knowledge about who or what I would be picking up. As the mission developed, I learned that I would be working with Colonel Crowe and his reconnaissance unit. Based on my past experience with picking up reconnaissance units, the window for the pick up normally covered a two hour period. This two hour window posed a serious danger because it increased the probability for detection of my boat crew and me by the North Koreans or Chinese. On the date designated for the pick up, my boat crew and I proceeded up the Korean coastal line behind enemy lines to the coordinates designated. Although small boats do not attract a great deal of attention, they do make some noise. Once my boat was beached, the hard part started. While waiting for the Marine Corps reconnaissance unit commanded by Colonel Crowe, my crew and I were very vulnerable. In fact, one might refer to us as sitting ducks. To help increase our chances for survival and for the success of the mission, I always used camouflage. To confuse the North Koreans and Chinese on our exact location,

I would have my crew camouflage our boat and set up two other separate camouflaged locations about one hundred and fifty yards apart along the coast. The other two camouflaged locations would be decoys. The North Koreans in the vicinity of the pick up would know that my boat crew and I were present because they had heard the noise from the engines of my small boat. I knew that the North Koreans would start frantically looking for my boat crew and me. In the past, North Korean patrols had walked within ten yards of my crew and me. Luckily, these patrols never spotted us. In reality, it was not these patrols that concerned me. With the element of surprise, my crew and I would have easily killed all the enemy soldiers in a patrol. However, if this occurred, our position on the beach would quickly be identified and a larger North Korean or Chinese unit would advance toward our position. If this occurred, it would force my crew and me to make an immediate departure without picking up the Marine Corps reconnaissance unit.

On this particular mission, my crew and I had established three separate camouflage locations. I had pulled my small boat as far up on the beach as possible. The camouflaged cargo netting covered the boat very well. It looked just like part of the sandbar or a rock pile. For defense of my position along the beach, I placed my point man with a machine gun about 500 yards from the boat along the main avenue of approach. At a distance of one hundred and fifty to two hundred yards from the boat, I placed two men armed with guns, and at the boat location I placed one armed guard. The North Koreans knew that we were on the beach somewhere. It is my opinion that on this mission, a North Korean lookout spotted and reported our presence in the small inlet. Although the North Korean and Chinese forces were uncertain about my small boat's location, they knew that we were there. As with all of my pick up operations behind enemy lines, my small boat was under radio silence to avoid detection by enemy triangulation procedures.

Suddenly, a North Korean fighter appeared over head. I could tell by the number of passes that this fighter made over our position that the pilot was unsure of our exact location. However, it was abundantly clear that he was looking for us. With each pass the Korean fighter would shoot those places that he thought looked like my boat or where my crew might be. In my mind, I knew it was just a matter of time before he would shoot my small boat or kill one of my crew. To the guard at the boat, I whispered, "Bring me an M-1 rifle and some clips of ammo from under the stern sheets of the boat." As he handed me the M-1, I laid down the grease gun that I had been carrying.

After loading the M-1 and checking the sights, I waited for the fighter to make his next pass. On the fighter's next approach, I aimed and fired. I must have led him too much because the bullets missed. However, on the next pass, the North Korean fighter came right over me, and I fired another complete clip. I had put every round into the Korean jet fighter. When the last bullet in the clip left the M-1, the North Korean jet fighter burst into flames. As the fighter turned away in flames, it looked like a giant shooting star. Within seconds the North Korean fighter crashed into the rising terrain across the inlet from our location. After the shoot down, my crew knew that time was of the essence. The shoot down would attract attention. Soon the entire inlet would be swarming with North Korean and Chinese forces. Luckily, Colonel Crowe and his men arrived at the pick up within a couple of minutes after the shoot down. Quickly, my crew got the camouflage loaded, and within 15 minutes after the shoot down, we were on our way back with Colonel Crowe and his Marines.

As I exited the inlet, Colonel Crowe moved up to my position, saying, "That was fine shooting that someone did." I tried to play it down, and I turned to Colonel Crowe and said, "It must have been one of your men, sir. My men only have grease guns, but somebody shot that plane down."

After dropping off Colonel Crowe and his reconnaissance unit, I headed back to LST 845. On this short return trip, I told my crew that our boat would be inspected within 15 or 20 minutes upon returning. The inspector would be looking for the weapon that shot down the North Korean fighter. I instructed my crew to dump all the extra weapons, rounds, and other explosive devices that we had for emergencies over the side if they would not fit in our special hiding places in the ship's armory. One of the hiding places for weapons in the ship's armory was a large barrel of cosmoline. Cosmoline is a petroleum derivative used for preventing corrosion. Those conducting the search for weapons would never check the cosmoline barrel to see if there were more weapons than there should be. The rules of engagement in effect for the Korean War were terrible. Under these rules, my boat crew and I were not authorized to fire at the enemy until ordered to do so. My shoot down of the enemy fighter was in direct violation of our orders not to fire, and if the inspectors found the M-1 rifle or any other special weapons that my crew had aboard the small boat, I would be court-martialed. At the armory every round of ammunition issued had to be accounted for or returned. As always, my crew returned every round issued unfired. With these rules for conducting the Korean conflict, the United States Forces were definitely at a disadvantage.

When my crew and I got back aboard LST 845, I learned that a forward observer had called in a kill for my boat. In addition, the forward observer had identified my small boat by number (1468). As soon as I stepped aboard the ship, I was ordered to report to the wardroom. I knew what was happening. While I was in the wardroom, a search was being made of my small boat for the weapon that shot down the enemy fighter. One of the officers in the wardroom said, "You know the person who shot down the fighter will get a medal." I responded, "They should. There is no doubt in my mind that the man who shot the enemy fighter down did some fine shooting, and if he had not shot the fighter down, my crew and I might not be here because that fighter would have blown us up."

Finally, a visiting Admiral standing off to the side in the wardroom, stepped forward and said, "Are you telling me that it was not one of your crew?" I responded, "Sir, we only had grease guns for forward observance. And we had 50 caliber and 20 millimeter machine guns. But none of those weapons were fired. It sounded like a Browning automatic to me that was fired. However, I was a pretty good distance from the shooter." As I made this statement, up walked the Master at Arms. He was with a big boatswain mate. The Master at Arms stated, "No gun or rifles were missing from the armory and none were found during the search of the boat."

What the Master at Arms failed to check was whether there were extra weapons in the armory not whether weapons were missing. The extra weapons that we took on the small boat easily blended in with the rest of the weapons in the armory. My crew and I had access to all the extra weapons and ammunition we wanted because we were always sent in to clear the beach, to bury the dead, and to destroy the equipment and munitions being left behind after a withdrawal. Each member of my crew had extra weapons that they had picked up. After the enemy aircraft shoot down, Colonel Crowe would not ride on anyone else's small boat except mine. He was superstitious, and he knew I had shot the aircraft down. In fact, when he learned what I said to the Admiral regarding the enemy aircraft that was shot down, he laughed, but he never told anyone that he knew that I had shot the aircraft down.

CHAPTER 15
LONGSHOREMEN STRIKE

The Longshoremen had gone on strike in Oakland, California, and they would not load out the Navy cargo ships. In fact, the Longshoremen would not allow anyone to load out the Navy cargo ships. When this strike started, I was involved in supporting another landing for the Korean War. The United States had been fighting the Korean War for over a year.

I was shocked to learn that I had been selected to go on temporary additional duty to load Navy cargo ships with supplies vital to the Korean War. Lieutenant Commander Gusparidge called me to the wardroom and asked, "Who do you want in your crew?" When Lieutenant Commander Gusparidge asked me this question, it was an easy decision for me. I thought to myself. Did I want to do this mission with someone that I had worked with for over three years or someone I did not know? I replied, "I want my old salvage crew that I worked with for over forty months." In response, Lieutenant Commander Gusparidge said, "Done." I provided Lieutenant Commander Gusparidge with the names of my former salvage crew, and he went to Rear Admiral Doyle to have them assigned to my mission. I was amazed that the members of my former salvage crew and I would be given temporary additional duty orders to Oakland, California. Twelve of the members of my former salvage team and I were certified crane operators. The rest of the men on my former salvage team had been riggers and divers during the numerous salvage operations that I had conducted in WEST PAC and in the Far East.

My orders for this mission came directly from Rear Admiral Doyle. These orders stated that upon my arrival in Oakland, California my crew and I were to: (1) clear the Longshoremen off the base, (2) keep the Longshoremen off the docks where the Navy ships were being loaded, and (3) load out the Navy cargo ships. After arriving at the Navy Base in Oakland, California, I presented my orders to the Navy Base Commander. The Navy Base Commander had been notified by message traffic that I was coming, and he had been ordered to provide whatever support I needed to accomplish my mission. I requested that the Navy Base Commander take me to the striking Longshoremen. During my meeting with the Longshoremen, I explained my orders, and I told them that my crew and I would use proportional force up to and including deadly force to carry out these orders. The Navy Base Commander said "You cannot kill the Longshoremen." To this statement, I responded to my crew, "Men, if they do not do what we say, kill them!" I did not know whether Rear Admiral Doyle would actually back me up. However, during a radio conversation with Admiral Doyle before I left Seventh Fleet, Admiral Doyle said, "I will back you all the way. I want you to load those ships docked at the Oakland Naval Base. You are authorized to use whatever force is necessary to remove the Longshoremen and to stop them from interfering with your loading of the ships."

After my statements to the Longshoremen about using the force necessary to accomplish my mission, they backed away and moved off the base as ordered. My crew and I went to the pier and in less than a week we had loaded the ten Navy cargo ships sitting in the harbor. We loaded the ships more quickly and efficiently than the Navy ships had been loaded in the past. We put the crews aboard those ships to work. In fact, they could not handle the gear and supplies as fast as we placed it aboard their ships. No one had ever seen cranes operated like my crew and I operated them. The cranes never stopped moving. I had three teams rigging and men hooking as fast as the boom came to the pier. I had my crew working in shifts. When one crew got tired, the next crew replaced them. It was a continuous process non-stop. I established an outside armed perimeter manned by machine-guns on the back of a jeep driving up and down the pier to make sure no one, including the Longshoremen, interfered with the loading of the Navy ships. I had ordered the men in the jeep to shoot anyone who attempted to interfere with the loading of these Navy ships. The speed and efficiency with which my crew loaded the ten ships in the harbor was a major factor which forced the Longshoremen to negotiate a settlement. Prior to my arrival, the Longshoremen had intimidated all the sailors and the Commander of the Naval Base in Oakland, California. My crew loaded the ships in the harbor as fast as they pulled up to the pier. We were loading the Navy ships with ammo, shells, equipment, food, and all the supplies needed for amphibious operations. Out of the seventeen members of my old salvage crew, twelve of them were the best crane operators in the Navy and perhaps the United States (including the Longshoremen). I never took a backseat to any other crane operators. Without doubt, I was one of the best crane operators in the Navy and perhaps the best in the United States. To be a good crane operator, you had to become one with the crane. You had to feel and hear it operating. Your reflexes and eyesight had to be outstanding. To be quick and accurate required the ability to judge distances and to have excellent eye, hand, and foot coordination. Unlike some men, I had a knack for being able to tell when a motor was straining. Just like anything in life you cannot put a piece of equipment in a bind and expect it to be successful at accomplishing the job.

At the time of this mission, I was just over 21 years of age. Like the members of my former salvage crew, if there was anything that I enjoyed better than eating, it was fighting. There was a bar called the "Hitching Rail" in Oakland, California. The "Hitching Rail" was located right outside of the Naval Base. After loading all ten ships in the harbor, my crew and I went down to the "Hitching Rail" to celebrate. A sailor named Leon Short, had been assigned to me. Short was not a member of my original salvage crew, but he had been assigned to me to support my crew by the Commander of the Navy Base. Short claimed to be the lead guitarist for country music singer, Ernest Tubbs. Anytime you get a group of sailors together, you have some who will stretch the truth as far as they can. I figured it was another situation where one sailor was bragging about out doing somebody else such as swimming deeper, swimming further, hauling bigger rocks. Bottom-line, I felt that Leon Short was pulling our legs about even knowing Ernest Tubbs much less playing lead guitar for the country music star. It was not long after that when someone asked me, "Hey Red, what did you do before you came in the Navy?" I laughed and said, "I taught Roy Acuff how to yo yo." When I said this, it teed Short off. In fact, I think this made Short very angry. Not long after this incident, Short came to me and asked me to go to the "Hitching Rail" with him. Unknown to me, Short had an ulterior motive for asking me to go the "Hitching Rail." When we arrived at the "Hitching Rail," Short took me over to Ernest Tubbs and introduced me. In fact, Leon Short's younger brother Jimmy Short was playing for Ernest Tubb's band. I was shocked. Leon Short actually knew Ernest Tubbs.

After my crew and I completed our mission, we were ordered to catch a ride on a Navy ship headed back to the Korean War theater. As luck would have it, there was a Navy ship departing out of San Diego, California. When I boarded this ship with my crew, I thought that I had it made. I was not in charge of the engineer room, and I did not have to worry about nothing or nobody. All I had to do was stand watch just like everyone else. However, by the time we got to Pearl Harbor, the First Class Petty Officer in charge of the engineering section had fallen through the ladder well and broken his leg. The ladder well where he had fallen was one of the forty foot ladder wells. Somehow the First Class Petty Officer had stuck his leg through the ladder breaking his thigh bone. At Pearl Harbor, the First Class Petty Officer was removed from the ship to receive medical treatment at the naval hospital. This left the Second Class Petty Officer and the Engineering Officer still aboard the ship. From Pearl Harbor, we sailed to Midway. Enroute to Midway, we lost the Engineering Officer. The Engineering Officer had to leave the ship to return to the United States because his mother had died. So in Midway the Engineering Officer left the ship to fly back to the States for the funeral. This left the Second Class Petty Officer and me as the only two Engineer Petty Officers aboard the ship.

In Midway, this ship suddenly received a change in orders. Our original destination was Tokyo, Japan. However, that was changed to include an intermediate stop at Enewetak Atoll. The entire crew was surprised. In addition, we had picked up an incredible amount of supplies at Midway for delivery to the Naval forces at Enewetak Atoll.

CHAPTER 16
HYDROGEN BOMB TEST

Since the Navy ship, which my salvage crew and I had temporarily been assigned for the trip back to the Korean War theater, was headed for an island called Enewetak Atoll, we became curious. Enewetak Atoll is located in the central Pacific Ocean approximately 2,500 miles west of Hawaii. My salvage crew and I were familiar with Enewetak Atoll because we had worked in WEST PAC salvaging a ship that had been split in half at Enewetak Atoll. No one on the ship seemed to know what the new mission was. The sailors in my salvage team and I wanted to know what we were hauling that needed to go to Enewetak Atoll. To find out, I decided to examine some of the crates. After opening several crates, all I discovered was toilet paper and old rubber tires for trucks and automobiles. Following this discovery, the Commander of the ship had a formation on the main deck for all personnel. At this formation, the Commander told everyone not to write home about our new mission or about what we were hauling. When the Commander said this, my engineering section and I just rolled laughing. I thought to myself. Do you think I am going to write home that I am on a secret mission hauling toilet paper and tires to some place in the central Pacific Ocean?

Even after this statement by the Commander of the ship, my crew and I had no idea that we were going to participate in the testing of a hydrogen bomb. Once we arrived at Enewetak Atoll, my salvage crew and I assisted in the off loading of numerous pallets of toilet paper and old rubber tires from our ship, as well as the cargo from approximately four other Navy cargo ships. During the unloading process, I operated the crane. Once off loaded, I had never seen such a pile of junk. All of the Navy cargo ships were full of junk just like the Navy ship I was on. Everything we unloaded was worn out. It was all junk. In addition to the toilet paper and old rubber tires, there were pallets containing bags of wheat and barley and bales of cotton. All these items were taken ashore and placed in buildings at set distances from the test site. I surmised the scientists wanted to see the effects on these items from the intense heat and radiation from the hydrogen bomb blast.

At the time of the explosion, my crew and I were getting ready to be lowered in a small boat by the ship's davits to the ocean water. I will never forget the day that the hydrogen bomb went off. I thought all the water would be pushed out away from the explosion site, but it was not. The water actually went toward the explosion site as though there was a vacuum at the bomb site. It was amazing to me that the water went toward the explosion site. We were warned not to look toward the explosion site, but even looking away from the explosion site, we could see the flash from the explosion reflecting on the water. You could actually see the flash go on out past us on the water. The water rushed toward the explosion for what seemed like several minutes. Then all of a sudden, the water reversed and came back. However, when the water came back, its color had changed from the pristine blue green found around the island to a muddy yellowish dirty color. The returning water from the explosion looked like the water in a hog wallow. The noise accompanying the returning dirty water was unbelievable. Even with ear plugs in our ears, the noise was deafening. It was a roar that I had never heard before nor hope to hear again in the future. Within about two hours, the water turbulence had settled down. Following the explosion, my boat was lowered the rest of the way into the muddy water. The mission for my crew and me was to proceed to the bomb sight to see what had happened. My crew and I were to sound the depth of the water at the bomb site where just a little over four hours earlier there had been an island. Above us in the sky were the remnants of the mushroom shaped cloud, which had been hurled upward by the explosion. My salvage crew and I did not understand the historical significance of this event. We had witnessed the detonation of the world's first thermonuclear weapon, the hydrogen bomb.

Several days prior to the actual bomb blast, I had walked over to the wooden tower where the bomb was staged. The bomb, however, was on a metal tower above the wooden tower. The wooden part of the tower was about sixty feet high. It reminded me of a fire tower. Above the fire tower was a metal ladder which went up like an antenna another twenty feet with a platform on it. The metal portion of the tower was where the bomb was fastened. The bomb was set about 80 feet above the surface of Enewetak Atoll.

While unloading the ships, I remember looking into the water. The water was clear to a depth of about 30 feet around Enewetak Atoll. Under the ships, you could see sharks swimming around. These sharks reminded me of seeing the schools of rotgut minnows in Brush Creek when I was growing up. One of the men on a ship we were unloading hooked one of the sharks and pulled it aboard the ship. Once aboard the ship, the man quickly cut two gashes in the shark and rolled the shark back over the side into the water. The cut shark started swimming, but almost instantly he was struck by two or three of the larger sharks as they tore huge chunks of the cut shark's flesh off. I had never witnessed a shark feeding frenzy. We watched the other sharks eat this wounded shark. It was as if they were starved. Not only did the sharks eat the wounded shark, but they started attacking one another. This feeding frenzy went on for several hours. The sharks appeared to be driven to this frenzy by the blood of the wounded shark, which had spread into the water. But the sharks did not limit their attack simply to the wounded shark. The sharks were swimming in circles and biting each other. As the number of wounded sharks increased, more blood entered the water. The blood seemed to draw more sharks from other parts of the island. If a man had fallen into the water near this shark frenzy, the sharks would have eaten him.

After the bomb blast, I was unable to find any sharks near the site of the former island of Enewetak Atoll. The blast, in addition to disintegrating the island, destroyed all the sharks, which had been around the island. I could not believe the entire island had disappeared. My crew and I were over the test site taking water samples, seabed samples, and mapping the depth of the island for three days. The cloud from the blast only lasted for about six hours. I did not realize at the time how great our exposure to fallout and background radiation was. I would estimate there were approximately 10,000 service members present around the blast from the Army, Navy and Marine Corps. All these service members had been secretly ordered into the blast site area.

At the site where Enewetak Atoll had been, the water was now over twenty fathoms deep (one hundred and twenty feet deep). Before the explosion at high tide, the island of Enewetak Atoll was about twenty feet above sea level. In real terms, the blast had disintegrated approximately 140 feet of the top of an underwater mountain. No longer were there two big islands, Kwajalein Atoll and Enewetak Atoll, in the Marshall Island Chain. Now only Kwajalein remained. Another site within the Marshall Island Chain, where the United States set off an atomic bomb, was Bikini Atoll.

We were not told anything about the size of the hydrogen bomb. Right after the hydrogen bomb explosion, the Commander of the ship that we were on ordered all members of the ships crew to be hosed down with salt water. I am not sure what purpose this wash down served since the ocean waters were probably contaminated by the fallout and muddy radio-active debris. I just accepted the hose down as part of the exercise. After being hosed down, my crew and I had to get dry clothes. All the wet clothing was gathered up and new clothing was issued. All total, the Navy ship we were on was in the Enewetak Atoll area for two weeks.

At the time, I did not know what future effect the radiation might have on me, my salvage crew, or the other sailors and service men who witnessed this event. Years later, after being examined by several doctors at the Veteran's Administration Hospital, they concluded that the tumors in my arms, shoulders, and back were a direct result of the radiation exposure from the hydrogen bomb explosion, which I had witnessed at Enewetak Atoll.

CHAPTER 17
LEAVING THE NAVY

M y three year voluntary enlistment in the United States Navy had been extended for a little over two years by the Korean War. The Korean War began on June 25, 1950, when over seventy-five thousand soldiers from the North Korean People's Army poured across the 38th parallel, the boundary between the Soviet-backed Democratic People's Republic of Korea to the north and the pro-Western Republic of Korea to the south. The Korean War essentially was the first military action of the Cold War. Some viewed the Korean War as the first war against the forces of international Communism. Finally, in July 1953, the Korean War came to an end. In all, some five million soldiers and civilians lost their lives during this war, and the Korean peninsula is still divided today. After the Korean Armistice, the United States Navy released me, and I was honorably discharged from the Navy.

About thirty days prior to my return state side to be discharged, I was tasked with checking out a battery problem aboard the Seventh Fleet Flag ship. As I entered the auxiliary engine room to check out the problem, the entire battery panel blew up. I was covered from head to toe with sulfuric acid. Some of the acid had gotten into my eyes, and I could not see.

From an earlier visit to the auxiliary engine room on this ship, I remembered that the engineering section kept a five gallon keg of drinking water (ice water) on a desk just inside the auxiliary engine room hatch. Based on this recollection, I knew this keg of water should be about fifteen feet straight ahead. I felt along the best I could. My skin and my eyes felt like they were on fire. The acid was eating me up. Finally, I made it to the desk, found the keg, removed the top, and poured the whole keg on top of my head. There was just one problem. It was a keg of vinegar. The vinegar almost took my breath away. Soaked from the vinegar, I slowly felt my way back to the escape trunk, climbed to the crew deck, and turned right to sick bay. When I reached the sick bay, a corpsman quickly put me in a shower with running water. When the doctor arrived, he wanted to know who gave me a vinegar bath. After I explained what had happened, the doctor finished cutting the remnants of my clothing off, gave me new clothing to wear, and treated the acid burns on my skin. Next, he cleaned and bandaged my eyes. The doctor told me that I was very lucky. If I had not been drenched in vinegar, the sulfuric acid would not have been diluted. Straight sulfuric acid would have caused far worse injuries to my skin and to my eyes. As part of my treatment, the doctor had me taken to the main deck each day to sit with my bandaged eyes facing the sun. This treatment lasted for ten days. When the doctor removed the bandages from my eyes, I could see.

It was hard for me to believe that I was finally returning to San Diego, California, to be processed for discharge from the Navy. However, before returning to San Diego, my ship, LST 845, had to drop off a thousand soldiers and their equipment at Fort Lewis, Washington. These soldiers were returning from the Korean War. Fort Lewis was a unique United States Army base. It was named after Meriwether Lewis of the famed Lewis and Clark expedition. We off-loaded the Army unit at the Navy port facility at Puget Sound, which was the closest port to Fort Lewis that could handle the heavy equipment. While at Puget Sound, Lieutenant Commander Gusparidge gave the entire crew liberty. During liberty, we learned that it was duck hunting season. My engineering section and I decided to go duck hunting. After killing a large number of ducks, the Canadians came down and tried to claim them. For duck hunting, we used 12 gauge shotguns without the plug. In a 12 gauge without the plug, you can get about 8 or 9 shells with one round in the chamber. A shotgun without the plug is a great weapon. However, I can understand why they have the plugs in the civilian shotguns used for hunting in the United States. If you cannot hit something with the three shots from a plugged automatic shotgun, you do not need to be hunting.

As LST 845 readied to sail south, the deck crew doing routine maintenance failed to properly re-fasten the anchor cable. This error was compounded when a new member of the deck crew inadvertently turned the anchor winch to pay out vice reel in. Since the anchor cable was not fastened properly to the winch, all the cable paid out. With the anchor and the anchor cable on the bottom of the Puget Sound Harbor, Lieutenant Commander Gusparidge was livid. He came on the announcer and yelled, "All divers make ready to dive."

Diving in the waters off the coast of the state of Washington was an experience. The water in Puget Sound was extremely cold, murky and dark. I was the first diver to go down. Although I was coated with cosmoline, I could feel the cold go deep into my bones. Thirty minutes was the maximum length of time that we could safely dive at a depth of two hundred feet without coming to the surface. While I was stumbling around in the dark on the bottom of Puget Sound Harbor trying to find the anchor or the anchor cable, the other divers on the ship were getting ready to take their turn. When I got my thirty minutes in, I was glad to get out of the water. However, I knew that shortly it would be my turn again. When it came my turn to start the second round of diving, Lieutenant Commander Gusparidge told the boat crew, "Take Petty Officer Duncan out about five hundred yards on the starboard side and drop him off." The boat crew did as ordered. After I got on the bottom, I started feeling around, and I stepped on the cable. I reached into my diving pouch and pulled out a balloon. Then I secured the balloon to the cable, and I pulled the pin on the CO_2 canister to inflate the balloon. When I turned the balloon loose, it shot to the surface. The ship's crew saw the balloon surface, and the boat crew was waiting for me as I came to the surface. Once aboard the small boat, the coxswain said, "Lieutenant Commander Gusparidge wants you back on the ship now." As I came aboard the ship, Lieutenant Commander Gusparidge met me saying, "I need you to get cleaned up. By the time you are cleaned up, the other divers will have the anchor cable ready to fasten to the winch. I need you to ensure that this cable is fastened correctly." I took a hot shower to get the cosmoline off. Then I reported with my tools. Once the remaining divers found the end the cable that the anchor was on, a red balloon was fastened to it. When the other end of the cable was located, a blue balloon was fastened to it. Next, I had the divers thread a one fourth inch steel cable through the anchor. With the anchor attached to the end of this one fourth inch steel cable, I took the other end of this cable and passed it through the eyelets of the winch. This might appear to be easy, but it was very difficult because I did not have the proper tools. After working for six hours, I finally coaxed the larger anchor cable into place with the smaller one fourth inch cable and secured it to the winch. Now, we were ready to test the anchor, anchor cable, and winch to see if they were working properly. On the first test, we gave the winch a thirty second run. I adjusted the switch on the anchor so that no one could break the cable or safety shear pins. Everything worked beautifully, so we pulled the anchor aboard. When the anchor came aboard, there was an octopus hanging on it. This was the only octopus that I saw during all of my dives in the ocean. The tentacles on this octopus were about 8 inches long. We laughed and joked about the little octopus, and how we were glad that we had not disturbed its mother.

While in the Navy, I was making a hundred and twenty-five dollars a month. Upon my discharge from the Navy, I was paid as a Third Class Petty Officer; however, I was actually a Second Class Petty Officer beginning on January 1, 1952. The pay for second class did not catch up with me until seven months after I had been discharged from the Navy. I knew that I had passed that Second Class Petty Officer test a long time before I got out of the Navy. I had a lot of friends in the Navy who had seen the results showing that I had passed the test. The net result was that even after my discharge, the United States Navy tracked me down and paid me the back pay that I was owed.

When I left LST 845 to be discharged from the Navy, I severed all ties with the former members of my salvage crew, the sailors in my engineering section, and all the crew members of LST 845. Lieutenant Commander Gusparidge (soon to be Commander Gusparidge) did his best to talk me into reenlisting, but my mind was made up. I was going back to Tennessee.